THE HOUSE TELLS THE STORY

HOMES OF THE AMERICAN PRESIDENTS

THE HOUSE TELLS THE STORY

HOMES OF THE AMERICAN PRESIDENTS

By

ADAM VAN DOREN

Foreword by

DAVID McCULLOUGH

DAVID R. GODINE · PUBLISHER

BOSTON

First published in 2015 by
DAVID R. GODINE, PUBLISHER
Post Office Box 450
Jaffrey, New Hampshire 03452
www.godine.com

LIBRARY OF CONGRESS CATALOGING-IN-PUBLICATION DATA

Van Doren, Adam, 1962-
[Works. Selections]
The house tells the story : homes of the American presidents / By Adam Van Doren ;
Introduction by David McCullough.
    pages cm
Includes index.
ISBN 978-1-56792-542-5 (alk. paper)
1. Van Doren, Adam, 1962- 2. Dwellings in art. 3. Presidents—Dwellings—United States—
Pictorial works. I. McCullough, David G., writer of introduction. II. Title.

ND1839.V34A4 2015
728'.370973—dc23

2015000579

SECOND PRINTING · 2016
Printed in China

TABLE OF CONTENTS

FOREWORD
by
DAVID McCULLOUGH

ADAM VAN DOREN is one of those people who has such enthusiasm for a variety of interests that he is himself invariably interesting. Added to this is a grand sense of humor and great talent as an artist.

He lives with his family in New York, teaches a popular course in watercolor painting at Yale, and keeps in touch with friends with illustrated letters that are treasures.

Adam and I first met at a reception in New York and found we shared a common interest in architecture and painting, and it was not long after that the remarkable letters began arriving, mostly about Boston and Yale to begin with.

The first of those letters chronicling his tour of the homes of the presidents was dated November 22, 2011. And clear it was from the start that he was off and running in grand spirit. There was nothing imitative about the letters. They were just as he is, refreshingly observant, good-hearted, entertaining, alert always to those details that distinguish one setting or one individual from another.

The homes of our presidents have, of course, been photographed time and again over the years, but with his eye for architecture and the human element, not to say his distinctive sense of humor, Adam presents these historical landmarks, as well as their former occupants, in a manner quite his own. He sees them anew, and consequently, so do we.

The letters kept coming. Of the forty-two presidential homes open to the public, plus a few that are not, he traveled to fifteen. Some he was seeing for the first time. Others he had visited before, but never to study and sketch.

He started with Franklin Roosevelt's house at Hyde Park, New York, on the Hudson. It was his first time there and I love that right away he singles out the formidable portraits of FDR's mother and wonders how it must have been for Eleanor Roosevelt to have had to face them every day. Empathetic note is made, too, of FDR's beloved Fala, and with understanding comment on what the little dog's companionship must have meant to someone with the weight of the world on his shoulders.

Setting foot in the habitat of a major historic figure, moving from room to room, paying attention to details, you nearly always feel another level of understanding of the human being who lived there. It is a degree of appreciation to be found in no other way, in my experience. And it is this that Adam's letters convey page after page, in both what he writes and his lively watercolor sketches.

In a total of four letters about Hyde Park alone, he gives full illustrative attention to the key props of the set, as it were — FDR's wheelchair and his Ford convertible. Including a small sketch of the room directory keyboard for the servants is to me an inspired stroke in that it speaks volumes about the scale of the house as well as the whole way of life there. And what a nice addition is Adam's full color map of the Hudson Valley!

"Mount Vernon was glorious to see again," he writes of the most visited home in America (over 500,000 people a year). And glorious it certainly is. He and I had talked at length earlier of George Washington's love of architecture, of how Mount Vernon can be "read" as a kind of three-dimensional autobiography, and marveled that nearly every aspect of the house, from its grand veranda to the choice of interior paint colors was decided by Washington himself.

Washington cared intensely about appearances — the appearances of everything from his clothes, his uniforms, the horse he rode, the carriage he traveled in, and first and foremost, the house he lived in. A man was judged by how he appeared, he felt, and a leader especially.

That no other home built in America in the eighteenth century looked quite like Mount Vernon was exactly as he wished, and the dissonance of the architectural details — the irregular spaces between the windows, the large cupola positioned off-center — give it a distinction all its own.

"I am continually impressed with the great harmony and proportion of the main house," writes Adam, who was trained as an architect. "The large cupola is a perfect scale, the triangular pediment in front is a brilliant touch."

In the nine-page Mount Vernon letter, dated June 26, 2012, Adam tells how, to avoid the heat, he started each day sketching on the site at 8:00 in the morning and how some days, with the temperature at 100 degrees, he would catch a bit of breeze off the Potomac River by resting on the veranda. "It was difficult though," he adds, "not to constantly think of the slaves who had to endure the heat from 'dawn till dusk' as instructed — or *ordered* to be more accurate."

More than a historical landmark, Thomas Jefferson's Monticello is an architectural triumph, a major work of American art, and in his time there, Adam comes to see Jefferson in a way he never had, as "a sort of American Leonardo da Vinci." It is a feeling I well know. From my own first visit at age fifteen and in the countless other times spent at Monticello over the years I have never not felt in the presence of what can only be called a grand-scale masterpiece. No matter how much one reads about Jefferson, no matter how many lectures on the subject one has attended, nothing compares to being "there on the mountain top," and no matter the season.

More and more I feel that every American, or anyone trying to understand America, should visit both Mount Vernon and Monticello and take time to soak them up.

Because of my own work, I looked forward particularly to how Adam would respond to the homes of John Adams, Theodore Roosevelt, and Harry Truman. And what treats he did provide! As the letters make delightfully clear, it would be hard to find three houses that so personify the men who occupied them.

Of Peacefield, the Adams house at Quincy, Massachusetts, Adam writes of its "quaint yet stately character," and that though the house seems small, compared to Monticello, its size serves as a reminder that Adams was from a far humbler background than Jefferson.

Then, too, the Adams house is the home of not one but two presidents, as well as an eminent Secretary of State, Charles Francis Adams, and one of the greatest of American historians, Henry Adams. It is like a geological cross-cut, whereby you see past times in layers.

Fair to say that in all these houses one feels acutely the presence of their former occupants, but at none more so perhaps than Sagamore Hill at Oyster Bay Long Island. Sagamore Hill is big, rambling, full of books and hunting trophies – elk and moose heads, elephant tusks – a house chock full of Theodore Roosevelt. There is never a question of who lived there.

A highlight of Adam's two letters from Sagamore Hill is his account of working alone out on the grounds one morning, concentrating on a watercolor of the house while trying to cope with the stiff winds of a November day. ("The ghost of Teddy?" he wonders.) Suddenly a voice speaks to him from behind. "Nice work. Keep it up." Turning, he sees Teddy himself – or rather, an actor dressed for the part, James Foote, who does dramatic recreations on the site.

The Truman house is far distant in Missouri and far different. It has no country estate name like Mount Vernon or Sagamore Hill, no stretch of lawns, but is simply the Truman house in a town called Independence. It is quite another kind of setting just as Harry Truman was quite another kind of American.

Truman never had any money to speak of, and at the time of his retirement from office, there was as yet no presidential pension. His only income came from his army pension, plus royalties from his autobiography. Further, he refused to accept speaking fees or to serve on corporate boards for large sums, feeling that any such "cashing in" on having served as president would be a disgrace to the office – a point of view that seems sadly to have gone out of fashion among more recent former presidents.

The tall, white, wood-frame house on Delaware Street, ample in size, was the home of Truman's mother-in-law, and all remained as she and his wife Bess would have it. The one exception is a small corner library off the front parlor where he had his reading chair, his books, his recordings of the classical music he loved – mainly Mozart and Chopin – and a cabinet for his whiskey.

Years ago, visiting the house for the first time, I was struck by how appealingly, humanly time-worn much of it was. Plainly, a new kitchen floor had long been overdue. But instead the large cracks in the old linoleum had simply (and quite effectively) been tacked back into place. And happily, according to Van Doren's letter, such human traces continue to be maintained. In Truman's corner library, he observes, "There are still finger marks on the wall beside his chair where he lifted himself to get up."

Running fully seventeen pages, the Truman house letter is one of his longest and one of my favorites in the way it also pays homage to the small town setting and includes a superbly rendered caricature of daughter Margaret Truman posed by the family piano.

Of those letters describing and portraying presidential houses I myself have yet to visit, the account provided by Adam that I like best of all is one I would have least expected. I can't recall ever having any particular desire to see the Calvin Coolidge home in Plymouth Notch, Vermont. Now I can't wait to go there, so full is the serving Adam provides of deft renditions in words and drawings of the "true Yankee" setting and the man it shaped.

Taken all together there never has been a tour of the presidential home places so refreshing as this, or one conducted by so congenial a tour guide.

David McCullough

INTRODUCTION

THIS BOOK began in 2011 at the Yale Club of New York. The author David McCullough, his wife Rosalee, and my wife Charlotte were having cocktails in the main lounge on the second floor. Surrounding us were full-length portraits of William Howard Taft, Gerald Ford, Bill Clinton, George H. W. and George W. Bush. Between drinks, David took me aside: "Adam, have you ever thought of painting the houses of the American presidents?"

"No, I can't say I have."

"Well, I think it would be a *great* book project for you," Mc-Cullough said. "It combines your love of history *and* architecture."

I considered this with little hesitation, clinked my gin and tonic with his scotch and soda, and asked, "When do we get started?"

I have always been interested in old houses, the way they were built, the stories behind them. But most of all, the people who lived in them. Who were they? What were they like? What did they do? My grandparents' farmhouse in Connecticut, with its uneven walls and wide floorboards, always fascinated me. As a child I spent hours in it, reading the books, looking at the art, poring over the photographs, studying the objects. There were the signed volumes by Thomas Merton, Archibald MacLeish, Robert Frost, and James Thurber (who sometimes included a drawing of

a dog). There was the old mantel clock I heard ticktock on lazy summer afternoons, while my grandfather napped and my grandmother gardened. There were the dried gourds on the windowsill that were saved every year simply "because they had no use whatsoever." And of course there was the rickety old upright piano which was always out of tune, but perfect for playing ragtime.

But how does this link back to the presidents? Well, because presidents are, of course, people, too, but their lives are so staged, so scrutinized, that it is hard to separate public persona from private. But to see where they live, how they live, and who they chose to live with, is to learn first-hand what makes them human.

I was determined to visit each house on a short list David and I devised. We never intended that I should visit every presidential home, but of the ones we did select, we followed certain criteria: that the house for the most part be architecturally interesting, that the choice be apolitical, and that I should be granted permission to visit it. In addition, we recognized that presidents have lived in more than one house in their lifetimes, so our choices were also predicated on whether a given residence had an especially intriguing connection to the presidents themselves.

David and I maintained a lively correspondence thereafter, and my dispatches to him were in the form of illustrated letters. Often I painted full-scale watercolors of each of the houses as well. (For those readers who are interested in *all* the presidential homes, along with their locations, the appendix includes a full roster.)

Until perhaps World War II and the advent of mass media, presidents have been elusive figures throughout our history. For most Americans, especially in the hinterlands, it was a foreign concept to even know what the president *looked* like, let alone where he *lived*. Before the Civil War, assuming you had access to newspapers or possibly a museum, you were limited to painted portraits, editorial cartoons, or the occasional daguerreotype, which were just then becoming popular. (Considering that few people in colonial times had mirrors, which were expensive, it is unclear whether the general populace even knew what they *themselves* looked like, save a blurry reflection in the well water). Mathew Brady's images of Lincoln were a turning point. The sixteenth president was Brady's great subject and no photographer captured a president's character with more artistry.

In addition, the president's privacy was sacrosanct, even with the press. As late as 1960, people were still unaware of Kennedy's debilitating back pain, addiction to painkillers, or, for that matter, his apparent infidelities. Few knew that Roosevelt was a virtual cripple through most of his four terms.

As to presidential homes, there was no National Park Service until 1916 to maintain and restore these historic residences or allow and conduct tours through them. Roads were mostly dirt, and even if you had the resources or inclination to seek out these homes, there were few commercially available maps to guide you. And who had the time? It took days, even weeks to travel on horseback, and farmers—who comprised the majority of the population before World War I—could rarely afford to leave their land. There were exceptions, of course, especially for people who lived in the vicinity of a president, and there are accounts of gawkers who would walk right up, unannounced, to Jefferson's house in Charlottesville and bang on his French doors to speak with him. These intrusions became such a nuisance that Jefferson would often escape to his getaway retreat nearby, which he built as a smaller version of Monticello, and named Poplar Forest.

Now visitors to these presidents' homes number in the millions annually. The sites offer trained docents, "discovery" centers, film presentations and gift shops with souvenirs galore. As a member of a Board that works with the Park Service to maintain the home of America's great sculptor Augustus Saint-Gaudens (not a president perhaps, but an artist who memorialized several of them), I can attest to the extraordinary effort required to curate and protect these sites, and to ensure that history is accurately preserved.

A *living* president's residence, however, is off-limits to the public and remains one of the few places on earth where he can find peace and quiet, assuming, of course, the presence of the Secret Service, which is supplied by the government for the rest of his life.

My efforts to visit—in person—the fifteen houses came from a conscious effort to get to know the homes of the presidents, and through them, the presidents themselves. It is tempting to opt for a "virtual" visit to these historic residences: many of the National Park websites offer slide shows, even video tours of the homes, and it would be a seductive alternative for anyone to see Mount Vernon's treasures without leaving their chair. But the rewards, I can guarantee, would be far less gratifying. For myself, I would rather feel the wooden bannister railing that Jefferson used at Monticello; recline on the back-porch that TR enjoyed at Sagamore Hill; sit at the kitchen table in Independence where the Trumans ate breakfast; and walk through the same front door as JFK did in Brookline.

The illustrated letters included in this book were an unexpected pleasure that began simply enough as an interesting way to graphically convey to David what I had seen. With each presidential home I visited, I grew more inspired; I added additional pages of watercolors, and created increasingly elaborate compositions. I began to see the missives as works of art in themselves. A great tradition of illustrated letters exists, of which I was well aware, going back to Beatrix Potter, Maxwell Perkins, Rockwell Kent, George Grosz, Andy Warhol, and Teddy Roosevelt himself, in letters he wrote to his children. In 2007, the Smithsonian Institution mounted an exhibition of many of these, entitled: *More than Words*, which I was enthralled by. In addition to the colored drawings included with the text, the handwriting in each case was extremely expressive, and created an intimate feeling with what I was seeing, more intense than a printed version.

The following descriptions and paintings of these houses reflect the order in which I visited them over the course of three years, not necessarily in the chronological order of the presidents themselves. They begin one blustery day in November of 2011 at FDR's home in Hyde Park, New York, and end on a hot, humid afternoon in October of 2014 at the home of Jimmy Carter in Plains, Georgia.

McCullough and I had already been corresponding for a few years as friends, and we both favor writing in script. David possesses especially good handwriting, and though he does not advertise it, he is a fine watercolorist (he initially aspired to be an artist, but decided he would rather "paint with words"). He does not use a computer; he has typed all his books on the same manual typewriter he bought in the 1960s.

I hope you enjoy the journey to these houses as much as I have. And perhaps it will inspire you to visit more of these private monuments to our shared history. As Philip Shriver Klein writes in his 1936 book about James Buchanan's residence, *The Story of Wheatland*: "The early lives of the presidents, eleven of whom first saw the light of day through chinks in the walls of log cabins, is certainly inspiring, but no more so than the story of the continuing simplicity of their lives after having held the first office of the land . . . practically every president after serving his term of office, was satisfied to return to his former home. These presidential residences . . . were not palaces, not castles. They were not designed to shed additional glory on their owners but were homes in the truest sense of the term." And homes, I might add, that are often windows onto their souls.

Adam Van Doren

I had rather be on my farm than be emperor of the world.

—George Washington

SPRINGWOOD, HYDE PARK, NEW YORK

FRANKLIN DELANO ROOSEVELT (1882-1945)

[term of office: 1933-1945]

PEEKSKILL, Spuyten Duyvil, Tarrytown, Fishkill. All Dutch names. These were the stops on the Metro North railroad heading to Hyde Park. From my window view, the Hudson River ran parallel to the train, its smooth, dark water shimmering in the morning light. This historic shoreline was FDR's heritage (the Roosevelts first settled it in the 1700s)—a source of pride, inspiration, and longing. "All that is within me," he wrote, "cries out to go back to my home on the Hudson River."

His once-large estate, Springwood, has lost some of its luster nowadays—family members sold off several parcels, and a shopping mall was developed nearby—but the "Summer White House," as it was once known, is admirably preserved. It sits comfortably back from the old post road to Albany (now a busy Route 9), with sizable hayfields creating a buffer from the din of SUV's. In an earlier time "traffic" was limited to carriages, Model T's, and the whistles of trains passing in the night.

A handsome façade of balustrades, arches, and columns greeted me as I entered the circular court. Springwood was designed to impress. An allée of lofty trees lines the original driveway, which to this day remains a dirt road. In the 1920s, stricken with polio, FDR had tried to walk this road. He bravely set aside his crutches, and stood upright; but after one step, he crumpled to his knees, heartbroken. Amazingly, throughout his presidency, FDR, his administration, and the press managed to shield the public from his disability. They carefully choreographed his appearances to hide the fact that he used a wheelchair, a deliberate concealment that would be impossible with today's constant and intrusive media coverage.

The back of the Springwood house faces a lawn that falls precipitously, like a ski slope, down to the river's edge. Large trees have since grown up where there once was a substantial view. My curiosity led me down the hill to the base of the incline. I painted the back of the building from a dramatic angle there, looking upward. The west side is a jumble of bays, porches, and chimneys—some of which were part of later renovations—and they contrast sharply with the classical symmetry of the front. Inside the house, the front foyer is an homage to Franklin: there is a statue of him as senator, a mahogany case with his stuffed-bird collection, and a series of marine prints from his days as secretary of the Navy. This was, after all, his mother Sara's house (she actually lived there with Franklin and his wife, Eleanor, for many years), and Sara exploited every opportunity to celebrate the achievements of her son. FDR was America's most famous mama's boy, and Eleanor could never escape it; a formidable portrait of Sara hangs in a main corridor of the house, a not very subtle reminder of who was boss.

The main living room is a large formal space with two fireplaces, gilt-framed paintings, and rows of tall wooden bookcases. It looks more like a mini college library, perhaps at Harvard, than a comfy place to curl up and read. But the Roosevelts were a learned, distinguished family who revered knowledge and knew their place in history. Rooms like this were meant to inspire, and elevated conversation was expected (though no doubt levity and good port were frequently welcome, too). Franklin is said to have composed his 1932 inaugural address here, and it must have been encouraging to be surrounded by the portraits of his ancestors—Isaac the Patriot and great-grandfather James—who flank either end of this room. Here, too, the president spent hours with his stamp collection, which is apparently one of the finest in America, and which, according to FDR, distracted him from despair during his struggle with polio.

Continuing my tour with ranger Kevin Thomas, I saw the custom-made elevator, just big enough for Roosevelt's wheelchair, which was installed behind the main staircase. Upstairs, in Franklin and Eleanor's sleeping quarters (they had separate bedrooms), I was shown an early version of the first domestic fire extinguisher. Franklin had them installed because of his intense phobia of fire. Periodically, he practiced his own emergency drills, teaching himself how to roll his body down the stairs, should he ever be alone in the house and need to escape.

Back outside, the stables nearby were a surprise treat, not because any horses remained, but because of a recorded audio tour provided by Eleanor, the "First Lady of the World." By pressing a small button near one of the stalls, I heard the genteel, aristocratic, and unmistakable cadence of her voice. (For many years, in fact, hers was the recorded voice of the "tour guide" for all the rooms in the house). It was FDR's father, James, who originally built the stables and who later added a riding track on the property, which Franklin enjoyed as a boy when riding his favorite horse Debby. Eleanor herself loved to ride, and wooden signs still hang on the stalls with the names of her preferred horses, Lady Luck and Patches. Eleanor would often ride to Val-Kill cottage, a stone house she built about a mile from Springwood. There she would gather with friends, host a clambake, and revel in dancing the Virginia reel. "The greatest thing I have learned is how good it is to come home again," she once wrote of this little sanctuary, where she went to live after FDR died.

The Franklin D. Roosevelt Presidential Library, in a separate building, holds FDR's desk from World War II. There are touching photos of Fala, his beloved Scottish terrier, who gave such solace to FDR (and the nation) during one crisis after another, from the Depression to Pearl Harbor to D-Day. Fala is immortalized in bronze at the Roosevelt memorial in Washington, DC, sitting proudly next to his master. According to the sculptor, my friend Neil Estern, Fala is the more popular of the two with visitors. It is a testament to this illustrious canine that he is buried at the Hyde Park property next to Franklin and Eleanor. And where else but in Sara's rose garden? It was moving to stand beside these tombstones. On my last visit there, the estate was eerily quiet, the tour groups had left, and a late afternoon chill had descended under a gray sky. Alone, I thought of the assembled crowd that once stood where I was standing, on April 15, 1945, for FDR's interment. Soldiers in uniform, members of the Roosevelt family, and political leaders from across the globe paid their respects.

When I arrived back home, I retrieved from my archives an invitation from the Roosevelts that was sent to my grandparents Mark and Dorothy Van Doren, both writers, more than seventy years ago. Its return address simply read "The White House," and it contained a small card that "requested the pleasure of your company" at a luncheon reception following Roosevelt's inauguration of January 20, 1945. The president would die only three months later.

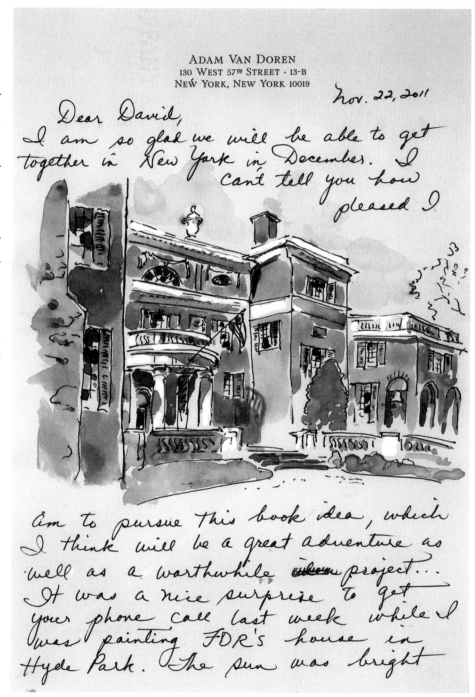

ADAM VAN DOREN
130 WEST 57TH STREET · 13-B
NEW YORK, NEW YORK 10019

Nov. 22, 2011

Dear David,
I am so glad we will be able to get together in New York in December. I can't tell you how pleased I am to pursue this book idea, which I think will be a great adventure as well as a worthwhile project... It was a nice surprise to get your phone call last week while I was painting FDR's house in Hyde Park. The sun was bright

ADAM VAN DOREN
130 WEST 57TH STREET · 13-B
NEW YORK, NEW YORK 10019

in the
it was
and I
froze to
to

sky but
a frigid day
damn near
death trying
render the
house. Luckily
I had brought along a
pair of Dickens-
like gloves, with
holes for the
fingers to stick
out. That at
least gave me
a fighting
chance... I
took a tour of
the house.

during the morning, and was intrigued
by how the house had been
outfitted with ramps and such
to accomodate Franklin's wheelchair.
The portraits of his mother are

ADAM VAN DOREN
130 WEST 57TH STREET · 13-B
NEW YORK, NEW YORK 10019

formidable, and I can only imagine
what it was like for Eleanor
to wake up to those   each
& every morning...   Being
a softie for pets, I   was
particularly taken   with
all the images   + lore
of Fala, who is   a book
onto himself.   I
was touched to   see that
he was buried next to the Roosevelt
tombstone in the rose garden, and
I loved seeing the display case
with his food-bowl and rubber
ball. One can   certainly
see how comfort'g   it was for
the president to   have this
little creature   running
around while FDR was   burdened
with the fate of the world.

ADAM VAN DOREN
130 WEST 57TH STREET · 13-B
NEW YORK, NEW YORK 10019

I took some time to see the stables as well where the guide

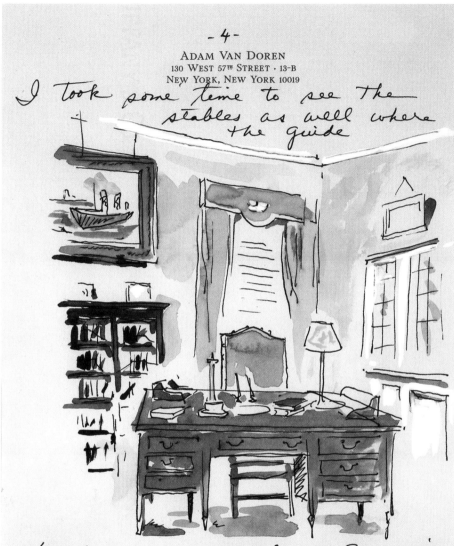

played us a recording of Eleanor's voice, with its unmistakable aristocratic cadences... In any case I will see you at 10:30 a.m. on December 15th, and best to you & Rosalee for Thanksgiving!

Best, Adam

ADAM VAN DOREN
130 WEST 57TH STREET · 13-B
NEW YORK, NEW YORK 10019

December 2, 2011

Dear David,

Sorry I missed your call. I'm so glad you liked the latest from Hyde Park. I tried you back on

your cell phone, but wasn't able to reach you. I went back to the FDR site yesterday, as I am trying in earnest to catch whatever is left of the

ADAM VAN DOREN
130 WEST 57TH STREET · 13-B
NEW YORK, NEW YORK 10019

warm weather. I worked this time on the side elevation which faces towards the Hudson. I have been struck, taking the train

along the Hudson, by how much that river meant to Roosevelt and his sense of his Dutch heritage. I learned that he designed his presidential library in the Dutch manner, as

ADAM VAN DOREN
130 WEST 57TH STREET · 13-B
NEW YORK, NEW YORK 10019

a consequence. It sounds like he was a frustrated architect, like Jefferson... Incidentally I met a friend of mine recently (she is now in her 47th year teaching at Vassar!) who gave me a copy of Eleanor Roosevelt's recording of her tour of the main house. As I

mentioned earlier, she can be heard in the stables, but there was a time when her voice was used to guide tourists through "Springwood."

Also, I was excited to discover that FDR's old Ford car is located in the basement of the museum.

ADAM VAN DOREN
130 WEST 57TH STREET · 13-B
NEW YORK, NEW YORK 10019

It is a treasure, and was retrofitted with all sorts of custom gadgetry that was, to accomodate Roosevelt's malady.

I mentioned to my friend Roger Angell that we knew one another, and he wanted me to ask you whether you remember his wife Carol Angell who used to work at American Heritage many years ago... Hope you had a great Thanksgiving

Best,
Adam

ADAM VAN DOREN
130 WEST 57TH STREET · 13-B
NEW YORK, NEW YORK 10019

December 20, 2011

Dear David,

A spell of mild weather late in December has brought me back to Hyde Park once more. I spent more time, on this trip, surveying the grounds. I walked across the fields in front of Springwood among the hay bales, which spread across the landscape like small

ADAM VAN DOREN
130 WEST 57TH STREET · 13-B
NEW YORK, NEW YORK 10019

sculptures. They provide a beautiful
fore
~~background~~ for the view leading out to
the main highway which borders
FDR's estate. I was curious about
the extent of the farm, and wondered
how much of it still belonged to the
house site. One of the rangers

explained to me that several hundred
acres were sold by the family shortly
after Roosevelt died in 1945 — because

many relatives needed the money.
Regrettably, some of the surrounding
countryside has been substantially
developed, with shopping malls + houses
springing up nearby. Fortunately there

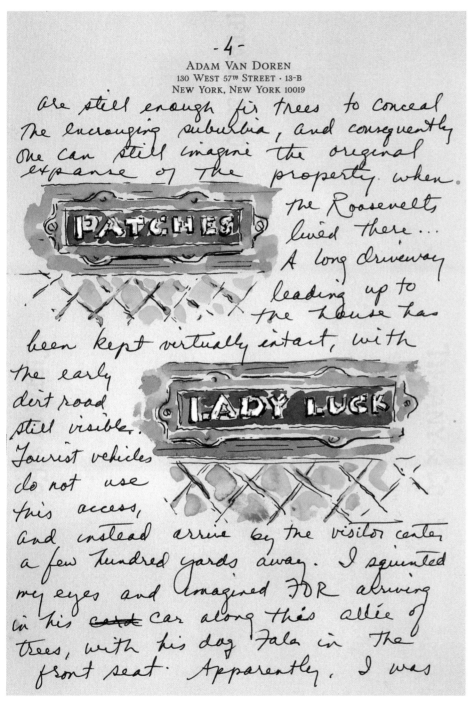

ADAM VAN DOREN
130 WEST 57TH STREET · 13-B
NEW YORK, NEW YORK 10019

are still enough for trees to conceal the encroaching suburbia, and consequently one can still imagine the original expanse of the property. When the Roosevelts lived there... A long driveway leading up to the house has been kept virtually intact, with the early dirt road still visible. Tourist vehicles do not use this access, and instead arrive by the visitor center a few hundred yards away. I squinted my eyes and imagined FDR arriving in his ~~cart~~ car along this allée of trees, with his dog Fala in the front seat. Apparently, I was

PATCHES

LADY LUCK

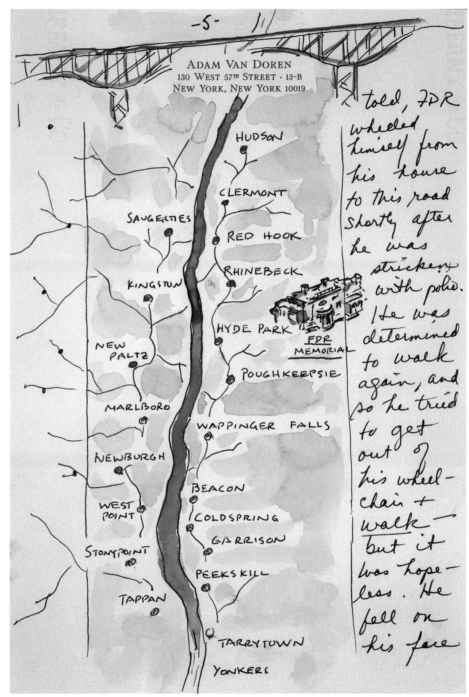

ADAM VAN DOREN
130 WEST 57TH STREET · 13-B
NEW YORK, NEW YORK 10019

HUDSON
CLERMONT
SAUGERTIES
RED HOOK
RHINEBECK
KINGSTON
HYDE PARK
FDR MEMORIAL
NEW PALTZ
POUGHKEEPSIE
MARLBORO
WAPPINGER FALLS
NEWBURGH
BEACON
WEST POINT
COLDSPRING
GARRISON
STONYPOINT
PEEKSKILL
TAPPAN
TARRYTOWN
YONKERS

told, FDR wheeled himself from his house to this road shortly after he was stricken with polio. He was determined to walk again, and so he tried to get out of his wheel-chair + walk — but it was hope-less. He fell on his face

ADAM VAN DOREN
130 WEST 57TH STREET · 13-B
NEW YORK, NEW YORK 10019

in a heap. He realized then
that he would have to live
with this crippling illness the rest
of his life... Later that afternoon
I took a path down behind the
house to a low area near the
Hudson River. It is a steep
incline, and I got a great
vantage point of what the house
looks like from below. The back
of the house is much less grand
+ much more "domestic" looking. There
is a porch looking towards the
mountains on the west side of
the River and the family must
have spent many hours watching
the sunset from there...
    Hope you + Rosalee have a
great holiday.   Best, Adam

ADAM VAN DOREN
130 WEST 57TH STREET · 13-B
NEW YORK, NEW YORK 10019

Feb. 15, 2012
Dear David,
    I hope this
finds you well
in Naples. I am
continuing full
speed ahead on the project, and
spent the day at Hyde Park last week.
I focused specifically on interiors and
was able to gain special access to
certain rooms through the Ranger

ADAM VAN DOREN
130 WEST 57TH STREET · 13-B
NEW YORK, NEW YORK 10019

Kevin Thomas. After filling out
the required permits to allow me
to sketch, I went to work. I began
in the living room which has heavy
woodwork and two handsome marble
fireplaces at either end. Over one of
them hangs a portrait of FDR's

ADAM VAN DOREN
130 WEST 57TH STREET · 13-B
NEW YORK, NEW YORK 10019

Grandfather, and the other has a
portrait of FDR's great-grandfather. There
is also a large portrait of FDR himself,
on an easel. It is somewhat uninspired
and apparently FDR disliked it. →

ADAM VAN DOREN
130 WEST 57TH STREET · 13-B
NEW YORK, NEW YORK 10019

His mother, however, was
pleased with it and
retrieved it from the
White House where it
might have ended up
in storage — or worse ...
The main hall, as you
enter the house, has

ADAM VAN DOREN
130 WEST 57TH STREET · 13-B
NEW YORK, NEW YORK 10019

several maritime prints
hanging on the wall and
a glass case housing
FDR's collection of
stuffed birds which
he accumulated as
a boy. A half-length
sculpture of FDR
sits prominently in
this foyer and for
some

ADAM VAN DOREN
130 WEST 57TH STREET · 13-B
NEW YORK, NEW YORK 10019

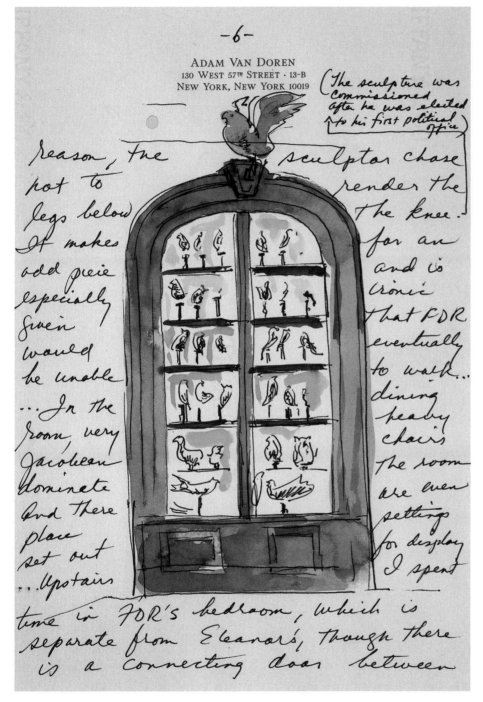

(The sculpture was commissioned after he was elected to his first political office)

reason, the sculptor chose not to render the legs below the knee. It makes for an odd piece and is especially given ironic that FDR would eventually be unable to walk... In the dining room, very nearby Jacobean chairs dominate. The room and there are even place settings set out for display ...Upstairs I spent time in FDR's bedroom, which is separate from Eleanor's, though there is a connecting door between

them. Eleanor's is much more spare, and looks more like a servant's room, with a low daybed and very minimal furnishings. Sarah's room is right next door to her daughter- in-law's; room; and there is a even a door that passes between them (!) ...while sketching FDR's quarters, the french doors blew open a couple of times, and the rangers and I were convinced it was FDR's ghost...

I plan next to go to Monticello, which I have been looking forward to. You mentioned once that you knew a contact

MAIN HALL · DRAWING ROOM · COAT ROOM · LIVING ROOM · SMOKING ROOM · SOUTH PARLOR · SOUTH PORCH · WEST PORCH · CHAMBER 1 · CHAMBER 2 · CHAMBER 3 · CHAMBER 4 · BATH 1 · BATH 2 · MORNING ROOM

SAGAMORE HILL, OYSTER BAY, NEW YORK
TEDDY ROOSEVELT (1858-1919)

[term of office: 1901-1909]

SAGAMORE HILL is an elegantly designed, perfectly proportioned Queen Anne house, a masterpiece of late shingle-style architecture. It is not, however, what many people expect Teddy Roosevelt's house to look like. They envision a Parthenon-sized log cabin with massive timbers and boulder chimneys. TR, after all, was the swashbuckling hunter of big game, the larger-than-life hero of San Juan Hill, the colossal face on Mount Rushmore. But this is Oyster Bay, not Mount Olympus. Roosevelt had titanic energy and a notoriously fiery temperament, but he was equally capable of tenderness and subtlety; he loved poetry (a champion of Edwin Arlington Robinson) and was deeply affected by the beauties of the natural world. His house is full of books, artwork, and souvenirs from a life that reveals and confirms a thoughtful, even sentimental figure. Of all the presidential homes I have visited, Sagamore Hill is perhaps most remarkable for the many original personal objects that are still present, and they provide revealing insight into his wide-ranging, if not contradictory, character. There is a gun room upstairs, for instance, where he collected Winchester lever-action rifles. He was fond of hunting big game out West; and yet, ironically, this was the same man who also founded the National Parks.

At the side of the house, there is a generous porte-cochère supported by sturdy wood columns. It evokes images of the Roosevelts arriving for the summer by horse and carriage from Manhattan, all six children in tow. I could only imagine what the sweltering heat of the city must have been like in 1890, with the redolent odor of horse manure—and worse—filling the streets. The cool shade of the large overhang and the sweet smell of the evergreens must have felt wonderfully restorative. It was the closest thing to air conditioning one could experience in the nineteenth century.

Entering the wide front hall, I felt as if I were embarking on a great adventure. The rooms on the first floor have a decidedly more virile quality than the exterior of the house: this part is pure man-cave. Mahogany beams and dark walnut moldings create a smoky atmosphere, like some back room of a Bull Moose Party gathering. The entrance to the large sunken living room, with its high vaulted ceiling, is punctuated by two great elephant tusks thrusting upward. Hunting trophies with jutting antlers line the walls, and animal skins cover the floors. I could name at least some of the slain creatures: elk, bighorn sheep, rhinoceros, wolf, antelope, moose, cougar. Where was my Panama hat and machete, after all? I felt like I was in the American Museum of Natural History in New York. But then again, and not surprisingly, Teddy's father was one of its founders.

The library parlor is less dramatic, and more intimate. I was given special permission to sketch it, as long as a ranger sat beside me. The supervision seemed excessive, but I was happy to oblige. Family portraits hung above three-quarter bookcases and a fireplace with arched brickwork. By the window was a rocking chair in which TR presumably relaxed; though I imagine, given his restless nature, he never sat for long. He was too busy plotting another safari, running a campaign, founding the Progressives. My friend Roger Angell, a writer for *The New Yorker*, once told me that Roosevelt suffered from manic depression and that's why he was always on the move, to distract himself from his own black moods. Kay Jamison, the author of *Exuberance*, characterized TR as "hypomanic on a mild day."

Roosevelt, despite his privileged, Gilded Age upbringing, was no stranger to tragedy. His first wife, whom he adored, died in childbirth (the same day his mother died). "The light has gone out of my life forever," he wrote in his diary. In order to submerge his grief, he requested, in true Victorian fashion, that his family never utter her name again. No doubt Freud, who emerged on the scene only a few years later, would have had a field day with this repressed notion of how to deal with loss.

After stepping out onto the back porch, with its sweeping views of Long Island Sound, I walked down the sloping green lawn and set up my drawing stool near the flagpole—the same pole which rises above the graves of TR's sons, Quentin and Teddy, Jr., who died in World Wars I and II, respectively. Some of the children visiting the grounds took a break from sightseeing and seized the opportunity to roll down the incline in teams. I imagined the house as it once was, alive with Roosevelt's kids. Teddy once wrote to Kermit in 1904, "[No] matter how things came out, the really important thing was the lovely life with Mother and you children, and that compared to this home-life everything else was of very small importance from the standpoint of happiness." (Kermit became a soldier and a businessman; daughter Alice became a writer and socialite; Archibald a distinguished army officer; and Ethel a World War I nurse who led the efforts to save Sagamore Hill).

When the coast was clear and the children had stopped careening past me down the hill, I began drawing my picture. I had just reached my stride with the pencil when I heard a deep basso voice behind me remark, "Good job!" Startled, I turned around and to my astonishment it was—TR himself! He was short and stout with spectacles, and wore his trademark wool vest and riding boots. In actuality, it was the actor James Foote playing the part. He visits the site once a month to entertain tourists, bringing the president back to life with an uncanny likeness. Foote is very convincing; he certainly had me fooled. In my mind's eye, I saw the *real* Teddy, bellowing with his hearty laugh, his squinty eyes, and his lust for life.

65 Commonwealth Ave
Boston, Mass.

November 14, 2011

Dear David,

You have indeed inspired me! Thanks
to your excellent idea of visiting Sagamore Hill,
I made a pilgrimmage to Oyster
Bay this past weekend and spent a
couple of days in its wonderful
surroundings, painting and sketching

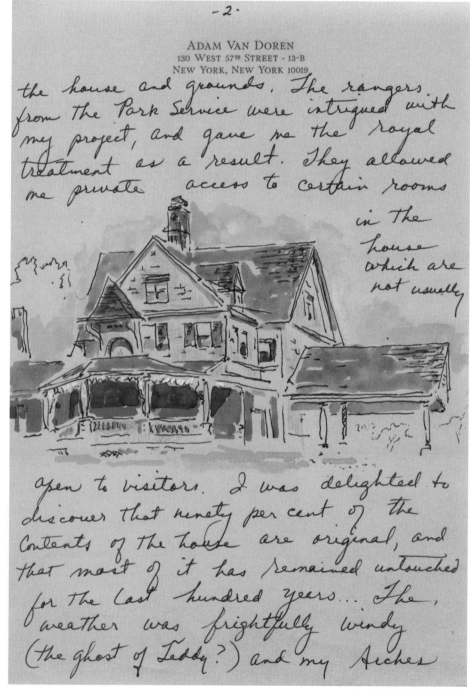

the house and grounds. The rangers
from the Park Service were intrigued with
my project, and gave me the royal
treatment as a result. They allowed
me private access to certain rooms
in the
house
which are
not usually
open to visitors. I was delighted to
discover that ninety per cent of the
contents of the house are original, and
that most of it has remained untouched
for the last hundred years... The,
weather was frightfully windy
(the ghost of Teddy?) and my Arches

ADAM VAN DOREN
130 WEST 57TH STREET · 13-B
NEW YORK, NEW YORK 10019

cold-press paper
sent flying with
of wind. But
with Teddy
beside me, managed
be productive.
a funny thing
as I was
watercolor,
behind me.
he
it
turned
who
see
dressed,
himself!

was frequently
each new gust
all in all, I,
indomitable spirit
to persevere and
Incidentally,
happened on Sunday:
leaning over my
I heard a voice
"Nice work,"
said, "Keep
up!". I
around and
should I
but a man
up as Roosevelt
He was

none other than James Foote (perhaps
you know of him) who is an actor

ADAM VAN DOREN
130 WEST 57TH STREET · 13-B
NEW YORK, NEW YORK 10019

who impersonates Teddy
for dramatic re-creations at the site...
In any case, it was nice to hear
from you from Washington, D.C. Hope your
medal ceremony went well... I continue
to be excited about this project and
will keep you posted. Best to you & Rosalee
Adam

North Room

Parlor   Hall   DINING

Library

December 5, 2011

Dear David,
I made it back
to Sagamore Hill
last week to get
some drawing done before the house
closes for renovations (according to
one Park ranger, they are going
to spent 6.5 million dollars on the
restoration!). I found the site
even more interesting this time,

now that I have visited Hyde Park. I
can see why Eleanor must have adored
her swashbuckling uncle — who could
match his charm, wit & boundless
energy? He seems to me what my
great-uncle Carl Van Doren wrote of
Benjamin Franklin: "he was a

ADAM VAN DOREN
130 WEST 57TH STREET · 13-B
NEW YORK, NEW YORK 10019

harmonious human multitude."

I am glad to hear that you had an enjoyable Thanksgiving on the Vineyard, and that Rosalee got a break from cooking this time around. ... I look forward to seeing you next week, and I thought we might get lunch after, at the University Club, where I am a member. It is not far from the meeting, and is located at Fifth Ave. & 54th Street.

Best Adam

ADAM VAN DOREN
130 WEST 57TH STREET · 13-B
NEW YORK, NEW YORK 10019

THEO. ROOSEVELT
EDITH KERMIT

TEDDY ROOSEVELT IS BURIED AT A CEMETERY JUST DOWN THE ROAD FROM SAGAMORE HILL

THEODORE ROOSEVELT SAID
KEEP YOUR EYES ON THE STARS AND KEEP YOUR FEET ON THE GROUND

OCT. 27 1858   JAN. 6 1919
THEODORE ROOSEVELT
MEDAL OF HONOR
LIEUT COL US ARMY
SPANISH AMERICAN WAR

P.S. I went to visit TR's grave nearby at Youngs Memorial Cemetery.

-5-
ADAM VAN DOREN
130 WEST 57TH STREET · 13-B
NEW YORK, NEW YORK 10019
THE LIVING ROOM AT SAGAMORE HILL

MONTICELLO, CHARLOTTESVILLE, VIRGINIA

THOMAS JEFFERSON (1743-1826)

[term of office: 1801-1809]

No HOUSE is more associated with an American president than Monticello is with Thomas Jefferson—and for good reason. Our third commander in chief spent roughly forty years designing and re-designing every aspect of his estate, from the mullions on the windows to the bricks in the fireplace. His taste, efforts, and inventions represented an ongoing personal initiative that eventually changed the course of American architecture. Daunting as it seemed, I recently tried to bring this storied masterpiece to life with pencil and watercolor.

My first instinct was to avoid the rear elevation; a view so well known it appears on the back of a nickel. I chose instead the side view, which is lesser known but equally pleasing. It is perhaps the ultimate compliment to an architect that his creation is engaging from every angle. (I later succumbed happily to painting a view of the rear as well.) But, then again, Jefferson had a good teacher: Andrea Palladio. From this Renaissance master Jefferson learned the art of proportion and harmony, two concepts that are deceptively hard to understand and even harder to concretely realize.

"Palladio is the Bible," Jefferson once wrote. "Stick close to it."

Like Villa La Rotonda in northern Italy, perhaps Palladio's finest achievement, Monticello beautifully blends into the landscape, a jewel on a hill that commands arresting views of the Blue Ridge Mountains from 360 degrees. Jefferson's location of the house is a testament to his aesthetics, and dogged determination. His detractors thought he was mad to build so far from a water source, but he would not be deterred and devised an elaborate system for hauling water from below the site. Today we rarely consider where our water comes from or how we get it; we simply turn on a faucet.

Never short on ingenuity, Jefferson invented scores of other contraptions for his house, including a dumb waiter, automatic French doors, and a writing machine that made duplicate copies of his letters. This facile wide-ranging mind of his was also an obsessive one. The intellect capable of embracing broad concepts like those in the Declaration was the same that meticulously recorded every seed he ever planted, every nail he ever made. What ultimately tempered Jefferson's genius, infusing and humanizing it, was his sense of humor. I thought of this when I saw the bed he built between two rooms that allowed him a choice each morning of waking in his study or his living room. Jefferson at Monticello, in his funny, farsighted way, had even planned for spontaneity!

Monticello, now a thriving tourist attraction with some half a million annual visitors and a state-of-the-art visitor center, is admirably run by Leslie Greene Bowman, director of the Thomas Jefferson Foundation, and her many associates including Susan Stein, Dan Jordan, and Ann Lucas, a researcher, who was an exceptional host during my stay. It is no exaggeration to say that I felt like a foreign dignitary on a state visit, such was the red carpet treatment I received. Special arrangements were made to allow me private visits of the interior at 7:00 a.m., before the throng of school buses arrived. I had the place to myself to study the artifacts of Lewis and Clark, the venerable busts of Franklin and Voltaire, the hoary Renaissance paintings, the hand-bound books in the library. I walked through the dining room and observed the elaborately set table with its shining silverware and wine glasses. If I closed my eyes, I could picture the food Jefferson would have enjoyed at various meals, the alimentary discoveries he made on his trips to Europe: waffles, which he first encountered in France while serving as ambassador; Nebbiolo wine, macaroni, and Parmesan cheese from his trip to Lombardy in 1787 to sample the culture and architecture; bouilli, soufflés, gateaux (again from France). Jefferson also relished the items he grew locally: olives, figs, mulberries, and fresh vegetables from his garden. Etched in memory is my matinal experience of walking through these rooms, in total silence, listening for the sounds of history that fill, faintly but always alive, every corner of this temple to the humanities.

Recently I was invited back to Monticello to attend a fund-raising gala. One of my paintings of the house was to be presented in a formal ceremony to a supporter of the Foundation, Peter Coolidge. Coolidge is a direct descendant of Jefferson, though surprisingly, not of Coolidge. There was a glorious dinner with lanterns under tents on the lawn, and amusing presentations by Pulitzer Prize-winning political cartoonists Mike Luckovich, Jim Borgman, and Mike Peters. In the distance Jefferson's architectural masterpiece was brightly lit by floodlights, its columns and dome glowing against the starry sky. I could just imagine Jefferson's wheels turning: "Ah! Electricity! Now *that's* an idea!"

May 30, 2012

Dear David-

I hope your Paris trip was very enjoyable. You are indeed fortunate to be fêted again for ~~only~~ all your stellar efforts. It is well-deserved.

→

I am thrilled to let you know that I have just returned from five days at Monticello, and I could not have had a more worthwhile, enlightening and worthwhile experience. The Jefferson Foundation welcomed me with open arms (thanks to you!) and I was given a wonderful cocktail reception at the end of my stay, at Fiske Kimball's former house at Shack Mountain. I exhibited some of my

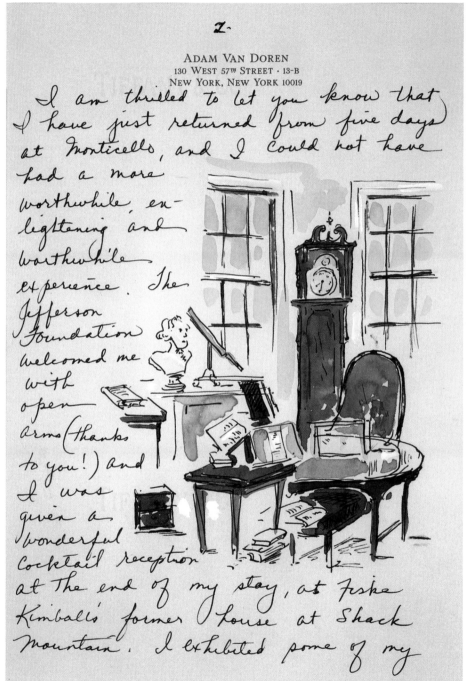

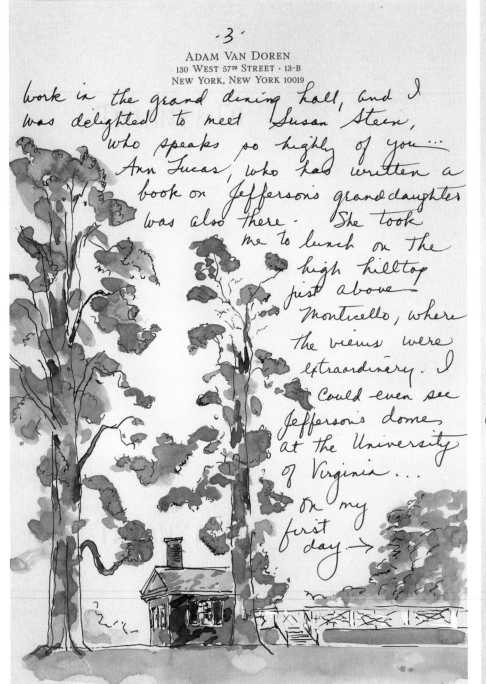

·3·

ADAM VAN DOREN
130 WEST 57TH STREET · 13-B
NEW YORK, NEW YORK 10019

work in the grand dining hall, and I
was delighted to meet Susan Stein,
who speaks so highly of you...
Ann Lucas, who had written a
book on Jefferson's granddaughter
was also there. She took
me to lunch on the
high hilltop
just above
Monticello, where
the views were
extraordinary. I
could even see
Jefferson's dome
at the University
of Virginia...
On my
first
day →

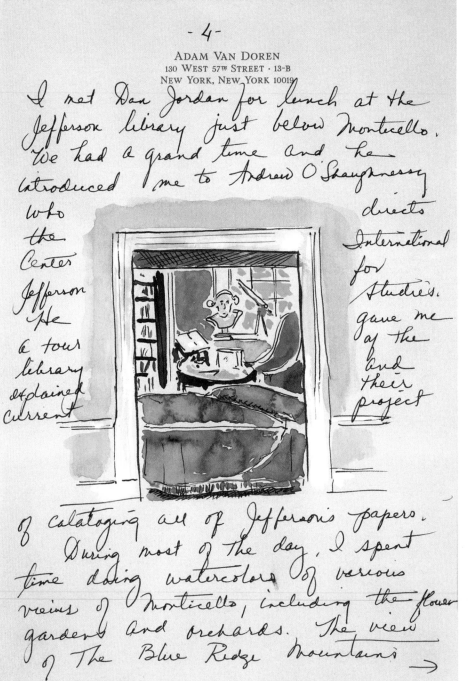

·4·

ADAM VAN DOREN
130 WEST 57TH STREET · 13-B
NEW YORK, NEW YORK 10019

I met Dan Jordan for lunch at the
Jefferson library just below Monticello.
We had a grand time and he
introduced me to Andrew O'Shaughnessy
who   directs
the   International
Center   for
Jefferson   studies.
He   gave me
a tour   of the
library   and
explained   their
current   project
of cataloging all of Jefferson's papers.
During most of the day, I spent
time doing watercolors of various
views of Monticello, including the flower
gardens and orchards. The view
of the Blue Ridge Mountains →

[42]

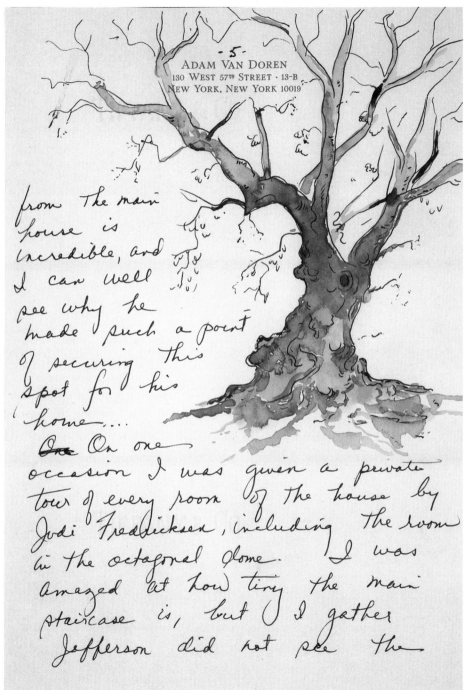

ADAM VAN DOREN
130 WEST 57TH STREET · 13-B
NEW YORK, NEW YORK 10019

from the main
house is
incredible, and
I can well
see why he
made such a point
of securing this
spot for his
home....
~~One~~ On one
occasion I was given a private
tour of every room of the house by
Jodi Frederiksen, including the room
in the octagonal dome. I was
amazed at how tiny the main
staircase is, but I gather
Jefferson did not see the

ADAM VAN DOREN
130 WEST 57TH STREET · 13-B
NEW YORK, NEW YORK 10019

practical need for "wasting" precious
square footage with it.
(After all, he probably
rarely went up-
stairs himself).

(...I spent a good deal of time
thinking about Jefferson's character
and I am struck by one great
paradox of his genius: on the
one hand, he was a man →

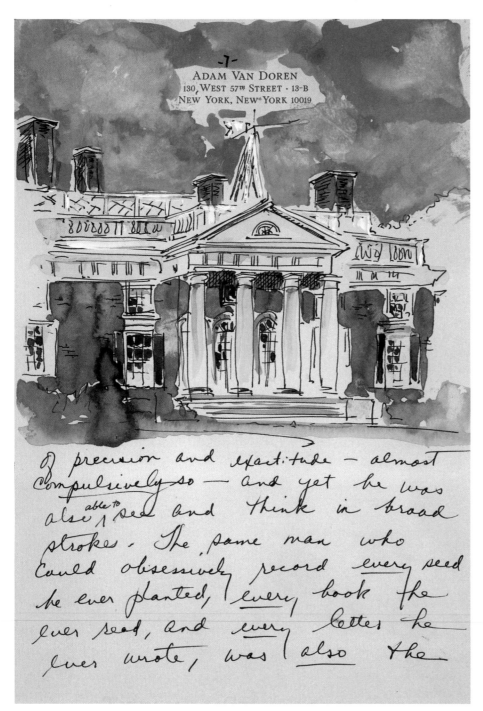

of precision and exactitude — almost compulsively so — and yet he was also able to see and think in broad strokes. The same man who could obsessively record every seed he ever planted, every book the ever read, and every letter he ever wrote, was also the

the man who could summon the big ideas for the Declaration Independence, etc.... His range of intellect makes me think he was a sort of American Leonardo da Vinci. I suppose there are many historians who feel the

ADAM VAN DOREN
130 WEST 57TH STREET · 13-B
NEW YORK, NEW YORK 10019

same way. ~~Incidentally~~, have you
written (same articles) on Jefferson
over the years? If so, I would
enjoy reading them. Of course
you have referenced him many
times in John _Adams_ & _1776_, to

be sure.
   Well, that's it for now. I hope
we get to see each other in NYC
this June. Best to you &
   Rosalee, Adam

MOUNT VERNON, VIRGINIA
GEORGE WASHINGTON (1732-1799)

[term of office: 1789-1797]

THE JULY HEAT in Virginia was getting to me. I had been sketching outside all day on the lawn in front of Washington's home. Long lines of languid tourists were filing through the house, as if on a conveyor belt. Dust was billowing from the bone-dry clay soil of the footpaths. The lolling trees above me were no match for the noonday sun, and I started to feel light-headed. All I could think about was the big, shady porch on the east side of the manse.

I took a shortcut there and found a Windsor chair under the eaves. The cool breeze flowing off the river was heaven. This panoramic stretch of the Potomac, with the rolling hills beyond, is the view Washington enjoyed as often as he could. Though he was rarely home during his presidency, it seemed to me that he would relish every moment on his porch that he could. A painting by Thomas Rossiter and Louis Mignot (*Washington and Lafayette at Mount Vernon, 1784*) indeed portrays a relaxed Washington, then retired, entertaining Lafayette, who is leaning against an ivy-covered column on the veranda. Martha Washington sits behind them, arranging a bouquet; children and dogs are playing in the sunshine on the lawn.

"I can truly say," Washington wrote in a letter to his friend, the Virginian delegate David Stuart in 1790, "that I had rather be at Mount Vernon with a friend or two about me than to be attended . . . [by] the Representatives of every Power in Europe."

Washington's residence was his haven because he made it so. Though Jefferson is well known for his design of Monticello, few realize how intensely Washington was involved with Mount Vernon. He selected everything: the siding, hardware, moldings, paneling, wallpaper, even the metal railing for his circular court. Though our first president lacked the polished education and genteel upbringing of his political counterpart, Washington was more than a rough-hewn soldier and statesman. He was also an aesthete. Born into midlevel gentry status, he closely observed Virginia's elite in order to learn how to raise his status in society. He memorized the lessons in *Rules of Civility*, an etiquette manual popular at the time, in order to acquire the gentlemanly arts.

"I would have the whole executed in a masterly manner," Washington wrote about his dining room, for which he specified a bold green color (the latest fashion) and chose side chairs from a noted

Philadelphia cabinetmaker. In a letter to his cousin Lund in 1776, he wrote: "The chimney in the room above ought, if it could be so contrived, to be an angle chimney as the others are: but I would not have this attempted at the expence [sic] of pulling down the partition. The chimney in the new room should be exactly in the middle of it—the doors and everything else to be exactly answerable and uniform."

The exterior architecture derives from Palladio's Italian villas, with which Washington and most of the South's educated elite were familiar. He specified flanking pavilions and porticos that emphasize symmetry on the façade. Subtler touches, like the cupola, the faux rustication, and the red roof are all evidence of Washington's refined sense of how to transform an ordinary farmhouse into a stately manor.

As the afternoon waned, I took time to explore the outbuildings surrounding the house, which create a sort of small village. I visited stables, the salt house, the spinning house, the blacksmith shop and the slave quarters. The last were particularly affecting. Families of four, sometimes five, were limited to one small room, with a simple fireplace, wooden bunks (with hay for bedding), a bare chair and table. This was the extent of the "amenities." Working from "dawn till dusk," they did not have the luxury of taking a break under a tree, or relaxing briefly on the grass. It is sobering to think that these slaves were likely among the best cared for in the country.

In the evening I got a bite to eat at the modern-day tavern nearby that serves dishes from Washington's day. The waiters were dressed in colonial costume, and it recalled my visits to Williamsburg with my children. I ordered the hoecakes that were essentially a flatcake made of cornmeal mush, but fried to perfection. They originated with the Native Americans and became a staple in Virginia and the Deep South. Nelly Custis, Washington's granddaughter, noted that the general liked this early version of today's pancakes "swimming in honey and butter" (I wondered if that also made it easier on his false teeth). Washington ate well at breakfast, and his dining room, with its tall Serlian window, was the setting for a feast at seven every morning. There was tea, coffee, hot chocolate, cold corned beef, red herring, cold mutton, and cold fowl, according to the clergyman Manasseh Cutler who visited in 1802. Dinner was equally hearty, with Washington eating like a veritable Falstaff. One visitor, Joshua Brooks, recorded in 1799 that the table was set with the following dishes: roast beef, mutton chops, hominy, cabbage, potatoes, pickles, fried tripe, and onions. Drinks included port and Madeira, and dessert offered mince pies and apples. To me, it all sounds like a prescription for heart failure, but then again Washington's version of daily exercise—long walks and hours on horseback—would put most of us to shame.

The last stop on my tour was Washington's tomb. A stone sarcophagus sits inside an open vault behind an iron gate. A woman dressed in colonial garb stands guard. Washington could hardly have imagined that half a million people a year would visit his home annually. There were barely that many inhabitants in all of Virginia in his time! But he did die knowing that he was universally revered and that he would be forevermore considered—no matter how inconceivably vast it would become—the Father of Our Country.

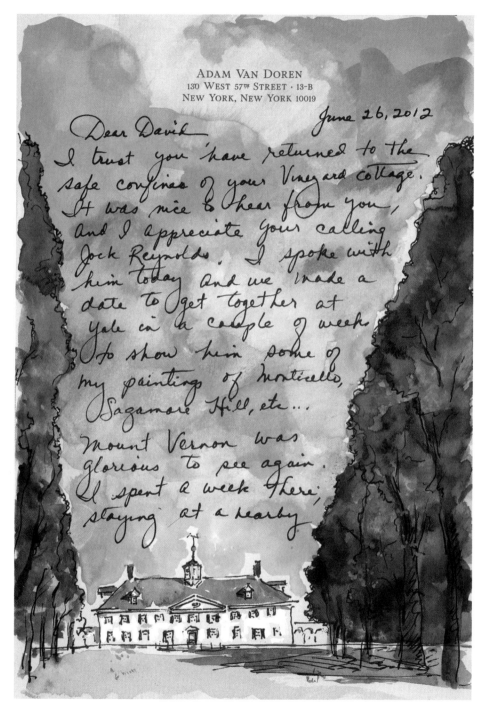

June 26, 2012

Dear David,

I trust you have returned to the safe confines of your Vineyard cottage. It was nice to hear from you, and I appreciate your calling Jock Reynolds. I spoke with him today and we made a date to get together at Yale in a couple of weeks to show him some of my paintings of Monticello, Sagamore Hill, etc...

Mount Vernon was glorious to see again. I spent a week there, staying at a nearby

inn and "commuting" back and forth each day, starting at 8 AM, so as to avoid the heat. It got to be 100 degrees on some days. Fortunately there was always a nice breeze off the Potomac. It was difficult, though, not to constantly think of the

slaves who had to endure the heat from "dawn till dusk" as instructed, or ordered to be more accurate. I read much of Ron Chernow's

new biography of Washington on the train down to Virginia, and it was interesting to see how many references Washington made in his letters to the moral evils of slavery. Clearly, like Jefferson, he could not readily reconcile its "practical" necessity.

ADAM VAN DOREN
130 WEST 57TH STREET · 13-B
NEW YORK, NEW YORK 10019

... (I was interested to also read how adamant Lafayette was that Washington follow Europe and set an example by freeing these men & women) ... Between sketching sessions, I spent a good deal of time sitting on a chair on Washington's back porch, looking across to Maryland on the other shore. I kept thinking of the comment you made to me that this large veranda, with its high columns, was an innovation of Washington's and that there was very little

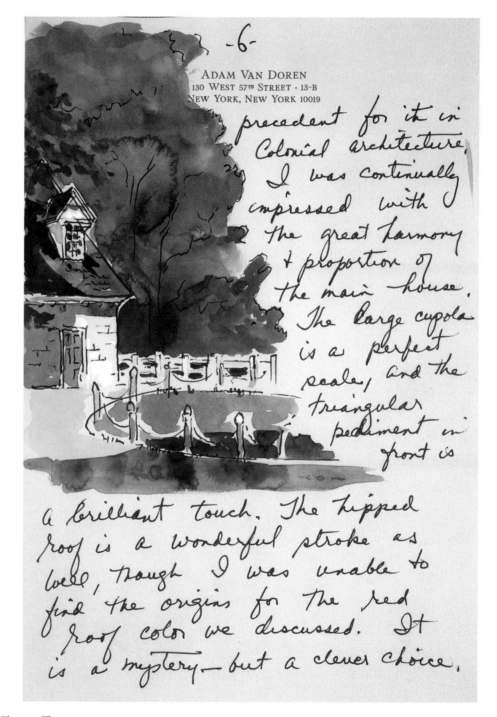

precedent for it in Colonial architecture. I was continually impressed with the great harmony & proportion of the main house. The large cupola is a perfect scale, and the triangular pediment in front is a brilliant touch. The hipped roof is a wonderful stroke as well, though I was unable to find the origins for the red roof color we discussed. It is a mystery—but a clever choice.

ADAM VAN DOREN
130 WEST 57TH STREET · 13-B
NEW YORK, NEW YORK 10019

I enjoyed painting the grounds and out buildings. The estate has the feel of a small village. Similar small structures must have also existed at Monticello, but they seem to have fallen down for the most part...

The last time I saw Mount Vernon it was during the early spring a few years ago, and I did not get to see how

ADAM VAN DOREN
130 WEST 57TH STREET · 13-B
NEW YORK, NEW YORK 10019

verdant the gardens look during the summer months. Flowers were in bloom everywhere you looked.

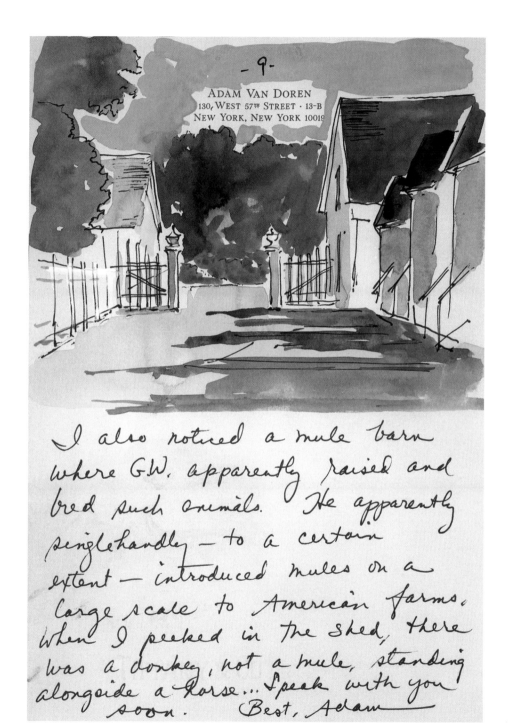

ADAM VAN DOREN
130, WEST 57TH STREET · 13-B
NEW YORK, NEW YORK 10019

I also noticed a mule barn
where G.W. apparently raised and
bred such animals. He apparently
singlehandedly — to a certain
extent — introduced mules on a
large scale to American farms.
When I peeked in the shed, there
was a donkey, not a mule, standing
alongside a horse... Speak with you
soon. Best, Adam

PEACEFIELD, QUINCY, MASSACHUSETTS

JOHN ADAMS (1735-1826)

[term of office: 1797-1801]

JOHN QUINCY ADAMS (1767-1848)

[term of office: 1825-1829]

THE WORDS on the swinging sign, just above the front gate, were the first thing I noticed: "It is but the farm of a Patriot." Humbler words were never spoken, and from our second president no less. But John Adams, hero of our republic, always thought of himself as a simple man, in the best sense of the term. The house he lived in is testimony to his self-image. It is modest, and practical, even homely. It is also handsomely decorated and appointed, but without the excesses and frippery a frugal Yankee would disdain. And though it commands a stately, dignified presence on Franklin Street, it has none of the grandeur of the homes of Adams's great contemporaries: Washington, Madison, or Jefferson. There are no columns or pediments or friezes. Much of the more elaborate furniture, such as a Louis XV sofa and a Dutch four-poster bed, is from acquisitions Adams made while in Holland during his ambassadorship to the Netherlands from 1780 to 1782. It made me think of his sea voyages across the Atlantic, which usually took a month, if you were lucky, and which were notoriously subject to filth, disease, and pirates.

To be sure, Adams was not as wealthy as his contemporaries at the Constitutional Convention, but primarily he was a man of principle (he had the means, for instance, to own slaves, but chose not to) who did not yearn for more than a comfortable place to dwell, a tranquil sanctuary in which to dream. In response once to a letter from his wife Abigail, who had asked him about his progress with the Declaration, he replied, "I am not writing at the moment. I am just spending the next three days *thinking*." Adams was a gifted wordsmith, and his recorded observations of the Convention in Philadelphia are of high literary value. His voluminous correspondence throughout his career is one of the great treasures of American history (his letters to Jefferson alone number in the thousands), and the exchanges reveal much about a man who alternated between intense vanity and deep insecurity. Like Walt Whitman years later, Adams often obsessed about himself. While looking in a mirror once, he wrote a self-critical portrait: "I am but an ordinary man. The Times alone have destined me to Fame--and even these have not been able to give me, much . . . Yet some great Events, some mean Hypocrisies, have at Times, thrown this Assemblage of Sloth, Sleep and littleness into Rage a little like a Lion."

Recently I read more of the letters between John and Abigail, and it was enlightening to discover what a groundbreaking feminist she was. "Remember, all men would be tyrants if they could," wrote Abigail to John on March 31, 1776. "If particular care and attention is not paid to the ladies, we are determined to foment a rebellion, and will not hold ourselves bound by any laws in which we have no voice or representation." And this was 150 years before women's suffrage!

Abigail commanded John's attention, and he often acknowledges his respect for her substantial intellect. His sensitivity toward her distinguishes our early president from many of his contemporaries who rarely considered their wives as much more than means to bear their children. Abigail was also in charge of much of the finances of their farm, which was a responsibility unusual for women of that time, and it reminded me that Peacefield was every bit as much her house as his. The wisteria she planted on the front porch is still growing after nearly two hundred years.

Outside, I found shade under an old tree in the garden by the house. To my left was an outbuilding that houses the library of John Quincy Adams, our sixth chief executive. It was built in stone, by his son Charles Francis Adams, to ensure it could not be destroyed by fire. To my right, tour groups lined up in front of the main house's ivy-covered veranda, eager to get a glimpse inside the homestead. The rooms in the residence are New England Colonial at their best, and the parlors include several portraits of Adams's ancestors, among the original settlers of Braintree (as Quincy was once known). In an upstairs room is the wing chair where John Adams spent his last night. It was July 4, 1826, fifty years to the day after the signing of the Declaration. Adams was too old and tired to take part in the festivities, so instead he welcomed some members of the press into his home. "What would you like to say to the people on this historic day?" one reporter asked.

"Liberty forever!" Adams responded.

"Is there anything more you would like to add?" the reporter continued.

"Not one word more," Adams said. He died later that night, within just hours of the death of his old friend at Monticello.

About a mile away, two other historic houses associated with this site are accessible to the public. One of the National Park rangers kindly offered to drive me to see them, and it was worth the trip. Humble as could be, these two clapboard saltboxes stand almost toe-to-toe on the edge of a small lot. One was the house in which John Adams was born; the other was the house he and Abigail purchased shortly after they were married—and it was there that John Quincy was born. The "new" house had space on the first floor for John Adams's law office, and I was pleased to see his writing desk still intact. (I stood next to it and considered how Adams, at five foot seven, was more than a head shorter than me.) To my chagrin, it was difficult to overlook the CVS across the street and the loud noise of traffic where once there had been open fields—how fragile our history is!—but I was grateful I could place my hand on the same walls and touch the same wood that two of our greatest presidents had also touched.

John Quincy would eventually inherit and inhabit Peacefield, as would his son Charles Francis, his grandson Henry, and his great-grandson Brooks. This succession of four generations in one house was relatively common in the 1800s, but is virtually unheard of today. Now Americans move so often they rarely plant roots. Though John Adams's son is not as revered as the Founding Fathers he grew up with, he was a distinguished president in his own right. His political education began early when he accompanied his father to Russia when the elder Adams served as ambassador. As a boy, he heard the roar of cannons at Bunker Hill and witnessed the burning of Charlestown. Later, as president, his acquisition of Florida from Spain in the Transcontinental Treaty of 1819 was one of many significant accomplishments.

Returning to my Marriott hotel, high above town, I wondered what the Adamses would have thought of their city today, with its dubious modern development and urban blight. They may well have appreciated the conveniences we now take for granted: fresh drinking water from a faucet rather than a well, toilets instead of outhouses, and radiant heat replacing drafty fireplaces. But given the pastoral serenity they would have to trade to live in the current world, it is not at all certain they would relish our military industrial complex. Perhaps they would have echoed the immortal words of Benjamin Franklin, when asked by a woman what sort of government America would have: "A republic, Madam, if you can keep it."

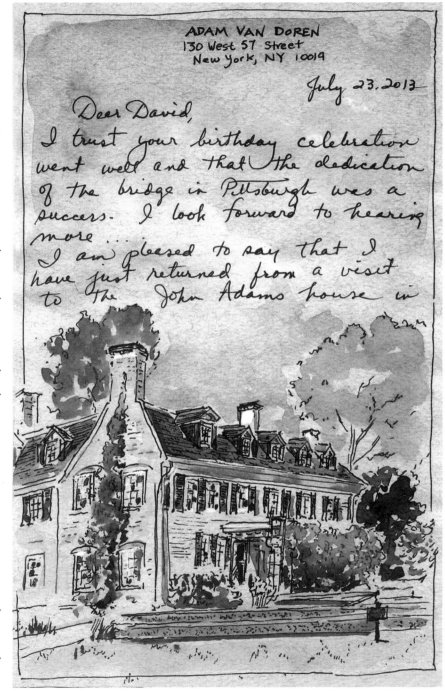

2

Quincy. The home was well worth seeing, and I was taken with its quaint, yet stately character, and its modest, yet noble architecture. Comparing it to Monticello, the house seems tiny, but it is a reminder that Adams was from a much humbler

"It is but the farm of a Patriot"
-J.Adams

background than Jefferson. The small saltboxes down the road, where Adams was borne and later lived with Abigail, are salient examples of his past as a Deacon's Son. The main property, or "old house," must have seemed

like quite an advance over his former residences. I was sad to discover that most of his original 180 acre farm is gone, and that the house now sits on just a few acres, but I am impressed with how subsequent generations of the

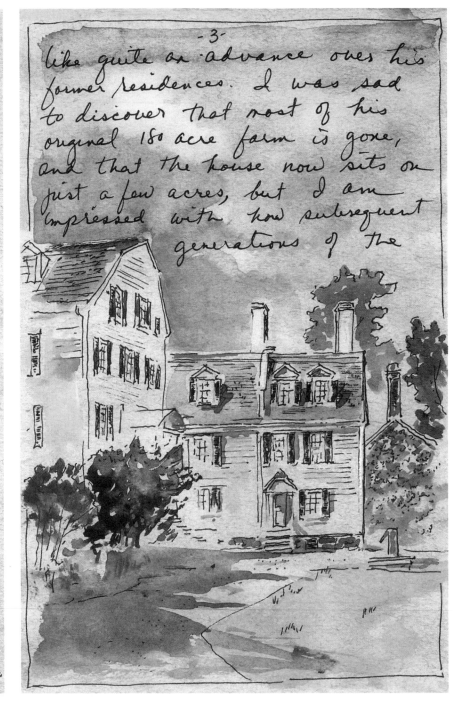

-4-

Adams family have managed to keep the main homestead intact. The Stone library, in particular, built by his grandson in 1870, shows a great desire to preserve the legacy of a true patriot... I was given a private tour of all the

Third Floor Bedroom

-5-

homes by one of the rangers in the Park Service who oversees the estate... On my second day there, a reporter from the Quincy Patriot-Ledger newspaper happened to drop by the site and spotted me drawing. He ended up doing a story in the paper which I can show you when we next get together... It is interesting to learn how the main house has

John Quincy Adams

John Adams

Abigail Adams

been enlarged over time. You
can still see the bend in
the roof, where the rafters have
lifted slightly on the front
facade at the location where
the addition was made.
I enjoyed sitting

7

On the front porch, which I
understand Abigail & John were
known to have sat to
en gain shade and watch
the passersby. The small
corner window on the left
of the front

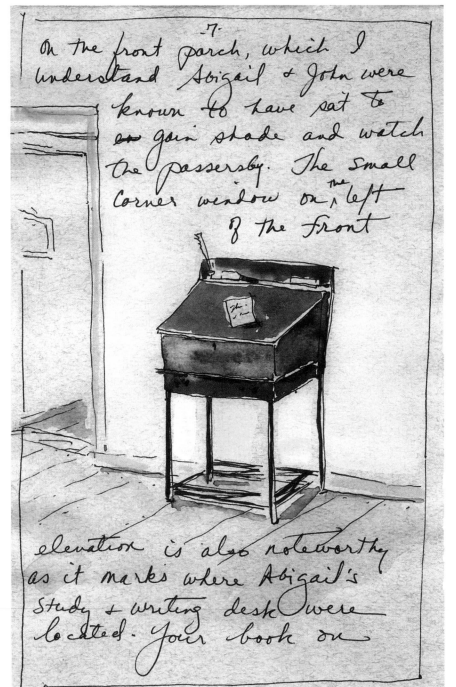

elevation is also noteworthy
as it marks where Abigail's
study & writing desk were
located. Your book on

-8-

Adams makes clear how much both John & Abigail seemed to share the same ambition in life: namely to forsake "fame and fortune" in order to

better seek a larger cause. I was also interested to learn that John did not fall for Abigail right

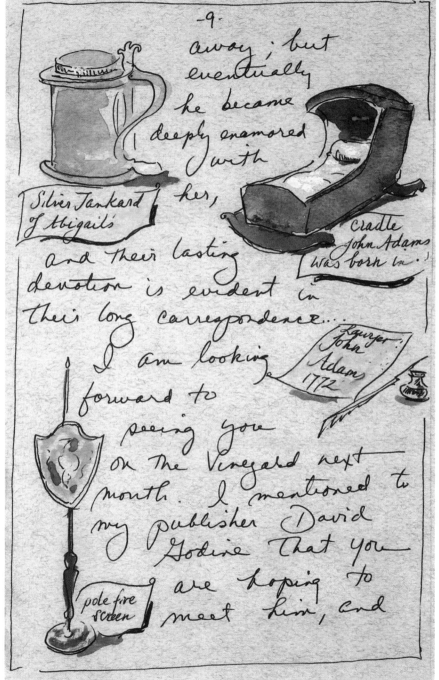

-9-

away; but eventually he became deeply enamored with her,

Silver Tankard of Abigail's

and their lasting devotion is evident in their long correspondence...

cradle John Adams was born in.

I am looking forward to seeing you on the Vineyard next month. I mentioned to my publisher David Godine that you are hoping to meet him, and

Lawyer John Adams 1772

pole fire screen

-10-

Godine is happy to come to the Vineyard to meet with

you and me for lunch or drinks on August 19, 20, or 26, or 27. Do any of

-11-

those dates work for you? All told, Charlotte & I will be there from August 18-28... Incidentally my daughter (a rising high school junior) has just finished reading your 1776 which she loved. She just won the top history prize in her school. Best to you & Rosalie, Adam

The "Stone Library" contains 14,000 books that belonged to J.Q. Adams

WALKER'S POINT, KENNEBUNKPORT, MAINE

GEORGE HERBERT WALKER BUSH (1924-)

[term of office: 1989-1993]

ON A COOL, blustery day in early November I arrived at Walker's Point in Kennebunkport, Maine. A few weeks earlier I had been cordially invited to the house by George H. W. and Barbara Bush. I was greeted by the Secret Service at a small shed at the head of the inlet and was escorted up the winding driveway past some guest quarters and a tennis court to the main house. The long, shingle-style building spread out in front of me with its assortment of irregular windows, dormers, and chimneys, each with a story to tell. Many a Bush family member—including Prescott, Jeb, George W., and Laura—has slept in these rooms. I thought of the conversations about politics, golf, Texas, shellfish, skydiving, oil that must have taken place here. It must be comforting for them to gather on this private peninsula where they can escape—albeit briefly—the scrutiny of the media.

The building's asymmetrical composition mirrors the craggy, meandering rocks that hug the shore on all sides. A strong roofline holds the architecture together and forms a handsome silhouette against the breathtaking view of the ocean. Walker's Point has been in the Bush family for over a hundred years (first built by Herbert Walker himself), and though the residence seems to have been renovated more than a few times, it has retained a distinctly Down East character, like the great homes in Bar Harbor and Camden. There is no mistaking the aristocratic life that emanates from it: of vacations from Andover, of sailing in the harbor, of scotch and soda on the terrace. There is the sense of dramatic history-making too, of fateful "summits" with Thatcher and Putin and Reagan. Bush presided over some of the more momentous events in American history: the collapse of the Soviet Union, the fall of the Berlin Wall, the unification of Germany, the Gulf War.

Though the house was closed for the season, I was left alone to freely wander the grounds and choose my best vantage point to paint. I was drawn to the water's edge, at the rear of the house, where the gables seemed to face the frothy Atlantic like the bow of a clipper ship. Unfortunately, my artist's eye got the best of me, and my chosen location forced me to navigate uneven, slippery rocks to find level ground. Sudden bursts of whitecaps slammed against the breakwater behind me. A Secret Service agent was gracious enough to offer me a blanket to keep warm. She then added, "Keep in mind that the tide rolls in at four p.m.!"

From time to time, my pencil and brushes slipped between the crevices of the rocks and, stooping over, I had to make sure I did not trip and drift out to sea, ending up like some casualty in a Winslow Homer scene. When the sun began to set, I moved onto dry land to paint my impressions of the front of the house. The sky was turning deep shades of orange and purple, and I had only an hour before it would be too dark to work. As I set up my stool, not far from a small putting green, I felt something uneven under my feet. Standing up, I noticed behind me a row of six or seven gravestones, each bearing the name of one of the Bushes former dogs, including the celebrated spaniel Millie, Barbara's favorite.

I was touched by this devotion to their pets, especially as I am inordinately attached to my cockapoo Winslow (named for the above-mentioned artist); and it demonstrated a warmer side of a family often portrayed as calculatingly political. It reminded me, too, of a tender letter I had received the year before from the former president. I'd sent him a copy of *A Yale Sketchbook*, a volume of my watercolor views of the university, where he had been Phi Beta Kappa, captain of the baseball team, and a newlywed. "Thank you so much for the book," he wrote to me in the shaky handwriting of a ninety-one-year-old. "Barbara and I so enjoyed looking through your sketches. . . . Memories, memories . . . thanks for sharing your great work with us."

Leaving Kennebunkport that evening, I stopped at Mabel's Lobster Claw restaurant. Quite by accident, I was seated by the waitress at the favorite table of the Bushes, with photos of their family above me. Through the window, I could see a sticker tacked to a telephone pole. It displayed an image of scion George W. Bush and read, "Miss me yet?"

Back in New York the next morning, I sorted through the watercolors I had completed of Walker's Point and picked out one I particularly liked and sent it off to George and Barbara. It was one of the pictures I had painted from the shore's edge looking up at the house, from below. A few weeks later, another letter from the Bushes arrived. "Thank you for sending us one of your very special watercolors of Walker's Point. . .It is a unique picture painted from a view that we don't normally see."

Whatever one's political leanings, I thought, it is hard not to appreciate the warm and generous response I received. I have written letters to many prominent people, far less renowned than the Bushes, and often got nothing more than a form letter in return. Was it just good breeding or good politics—or was it something in those lobsters?

ADAM VAN DOREN
130 West 57 Street
New York City

Oct. 31, 2013

Dear David,
 It was wonderful to see you and Rosalee in Boston last week. I am so pleased you could make my Childs Gallery reception and dinner afterwards... This past Monday I made the drive up to Kennebunkport to paint the Bush house at Walker's Point. Earlier this month I sent a letter to George W. to ask for his permission.

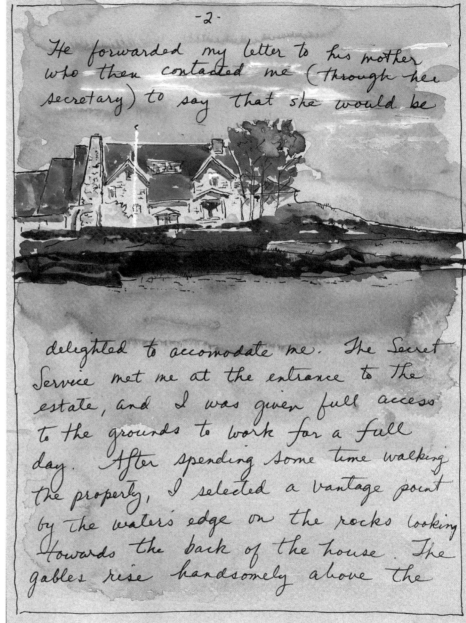

He forwarded my letter to his mother who then contacted me (through her secretary) to say that she would be delighted to accomodate me. The Secret Service met me at the entrance to the estate, and I was given full access to the grounds to work for a full day. After spending some time walking the property, I selected a vantage point by the water's edge on the rocks looking towards the back of the house. The gables rise handsomely above the ocean surf, and I managed to find a footing for my folding stool on the

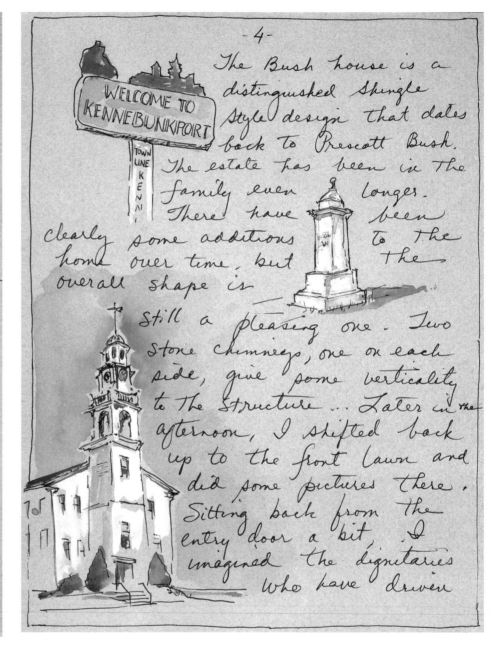

craggy boulders. The waves were splashing noticeably behind me, and I was aware that the tide would roll in later that afternoon. Though it was sunny, it was very chilly and windy, and I was forced to wear gloves and several layers of clothing to keep warm. At one point in the afternoon, a member of the Secret Service offered me a blanket, which was generous.

The Bush house is a distinguished Shingle style design that dates back to Prescott Bush. The estate has been in the family even longer. There have been clearly some additions to the home over time, but the overall shape is still a pleasing one. Two stone chimneys, one on each side, give some verticality to the structure ... Later in the afternoon, I shifted back up to the front lawn and did some pictures there. Sitting back from the entry door a bit, I imagined the dignitaries who have driven

up the driveway over the years,
including Thatcher and Gorbachev.
Looking up at the windows on the
facade, I tried to guess what

each room was used for. At one
point I got up from my stool to
notice a small row of gravestones
which have memoralized all the
Bush family's dogs, including
Millie... When it was time to
leave the site, Charlotte picked

me up and we headed back to
our hotel, The White Barn Inn,
which is a very pleasant, elegant
place to stay. Before we set
on the highway back to NYC,
we ate dinner at Mabel's
Lobster Claw which has
excellent chowder. We were
seated at the "Presidents' Table",
which is apparently where the
Bush family often sits when
they visit...

Charlotte and I hope
to see you in Stockbridge
next month at the
event for Wendell
Minor at the
Norman Rockwell Museum.
All the best,
Adam

WOODROW WILSON HOME, WASHINGTON, DC
WOODROW WILSON (1856-1924)

[term of office: 1913-1921]

WOODROW WILSON's house in Washington, DC, does not look like the home of a professor (which Wilson was, both at Princeton University and Johns Hopkins University), but it does resemble the residence of a president. A formal Georgian building near Dupont Circle, the house is made of brick and stone in a style reminiscent of the Knickerbocker Club in New York. Tall arched windows line the second floor and a semi-circular portico with columns marks the entrance. After Wilson retired from the White House in 1921, he and his wife Edith chose to stay in the capital. Wilson was by then a world figure, and though suffering the effects of a stroke, he stoically entertained various dignitaries and friends there for the remainder of his life. In the end, the native Virginian lived only four years in the house before he died, (Edith remained for two more decades), but it is full of myriad, matchless possessions garnered over his distinguished lifetime.

I visited on Veterans Day and was met that morning by curator Sarah Andrews, who had granted me permission to paint. I began sketching the front façade and set up my stool on the sidewalk across the street. A policeman in a patrol car drove slowly by a few times, and then he stopped. "Do you know where you are sitting?" I wasn't sure what he was after. "The building behind you is the ambassador of Pakistan's residence," he said. "Just so you know," and then he drove off. I interpreted this cryptic comment to suggest I should be careful of any bomb attacks, or some other mischief, although such portentous happenings hardly seemed likely on this quiet street during a holiday. Frankly, I was more concerned with the challenge of rendering this dim north-facing elevation, with no sun to brighten it. Architecture seems unduly solemn without light, even somber, so I did my best to breathe some lambent life into the structure using color and form.

At lunchtime I took a break and went inside the historic house, which is now a museum. I was treated to a tour by Andrews who escorted me to a large marble foyer, dominated by a substantial staircase. Andrews then turned left, and we entered a small study brimming with Wilson memorabilia. There was a framed case full of lamb's wool, sheared from sheep on the White House lawn when they still roamed the grounds. There was also a signed vintage baseball in a glass cabinet. Wilson was an avid fan of the national pastime, even during his days as a Princeton undergraduate, and I observed a photograph of him throwing out the first pitch of the home opener for the Yankees in 1916. In one corner of the room was an early version of the typewriter, which looked to me like an uncouth prehistoric animal.

Upstairs, a spacious living room greeted us at the top landing. It contains a large piano, which Wilson's daughter played when she visited, as well as some fine china and paintings given as gifts. Red upholstered Victorian furniture surrounds the room's edges and fill out the space. The effect is quite formal, and it was hard for me to imagine anyone spending casual time there.

The library is where I got a better sense of Wilson. It has bookcases from floor to ceiling, and his favorite cushy reading chair. On a back table sits a film projector, given to him when he was president. A frequent source of entertainment confirming Wilson's delight in movies, it a lighter side to a man who often appeared starched and humorless, in his tightly fitted collars and pince-nez. Wilson had a passionate side, as the love letters to his wives at-test. I read them in detail in Scott Berg's recent biography of the twenty-eighth president. He wrote to his first wife, Helen: "Are you prepared for the storm of love making with which you will be assailed?" Not a man as buttoned-up, apparently, as all that.

But Wilson was decidedly not all fun and games; he had a dark side as well. Soon after he took the oath of office, he ordered that all federal agencies be segregated, with African Americans relegated to separate restrooms and cafeterias. This was a loathsome setback for the early civil rights efforts, which, after Reconstruction, had allowed black government employees to work beside whites. The fact that Wilson grew up in the old South was hardly an excuse for the reintroduction of these racist policies.

In the afternoon, I returned outside to the back of the house, which has an elegant sunken garden, and where I became happily engaged in composing a watercolor of a set of French windows leading out to a terrace. Wilson was fortunate to have lived out his last years in such splendor. He never had much money but his friends were loyal to him, and this house, in fact, was purchased for him by his Princeton classmates. Not bad for a former college professor.

November 27, 2013

Dear David,
I trust you have returned from Dallas
by now and are getting ready to.
Have Thanksgiving with your family...
I have recently come back from
visiting the Woodrow Wilson house in

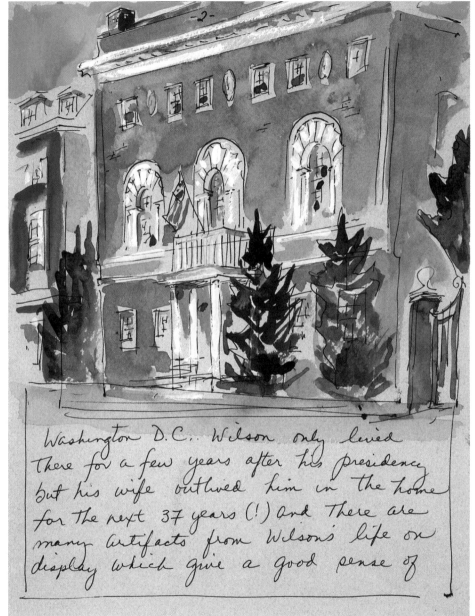

Washington D.C.. Wilson only lived
there for a few years after his presidency
but his wife outlived him in the home
for the next 37 years (!) and there are
many artifacts from Wilson's life on
display which give a good sense of

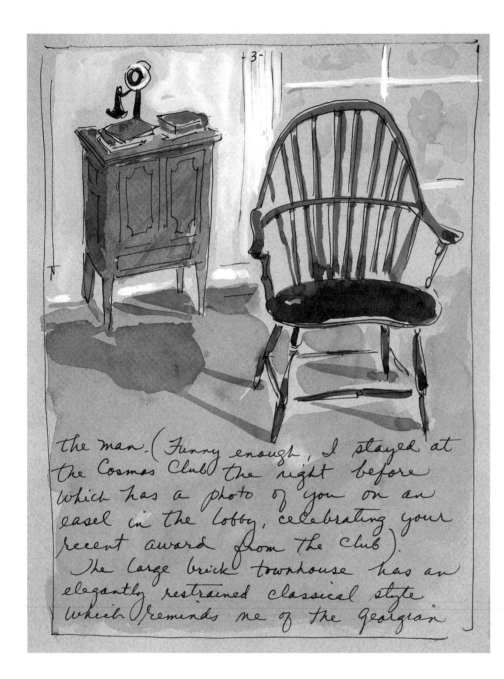

-3-

the man. (Funny enough, I stayed at the Cosmos Club the night before which has a photo of you on an easel in the lobby, celebrating your recent award from the club).

The large brick townhouse has an elegantly restrained classical style which reminds me of the Georgian

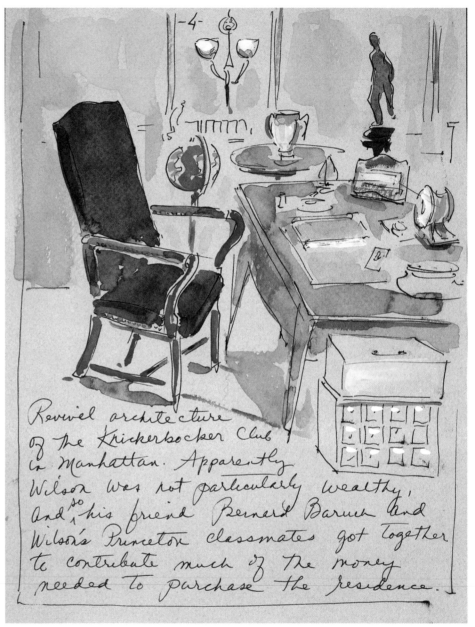

-4-

Revival architecture of the Knickerbocker Club in Manhattan. Apparently Wilson was not particularly wealthy, and so, his friend Bernard Baruch and Wilson's Princeton classmates got together to contribute much of the money needed to purchase the residence.

5

The curator Stephanie Dougherty and the manager Sarah Andrews met me at the front door to give me a private tour. The wide entry door leads to a formal stair hall with a study to the left which features some Wilson

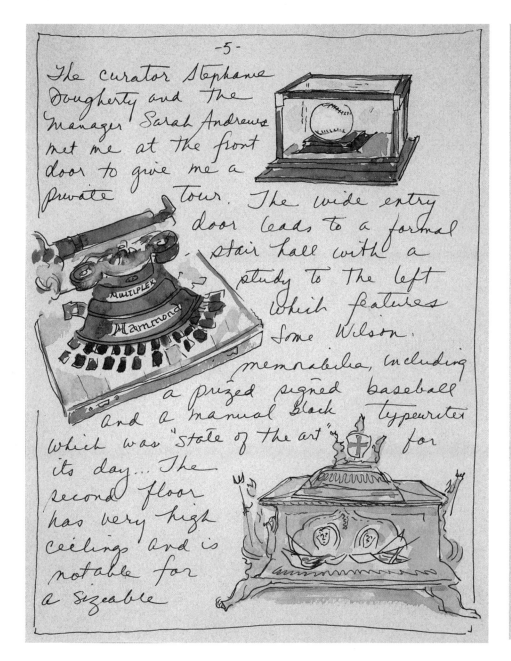

memorabilia, including a prized signed baseball and a manual black typewriter which was "state of the art" for its day... The second floor has very high ceilings and is notable for a sizeable

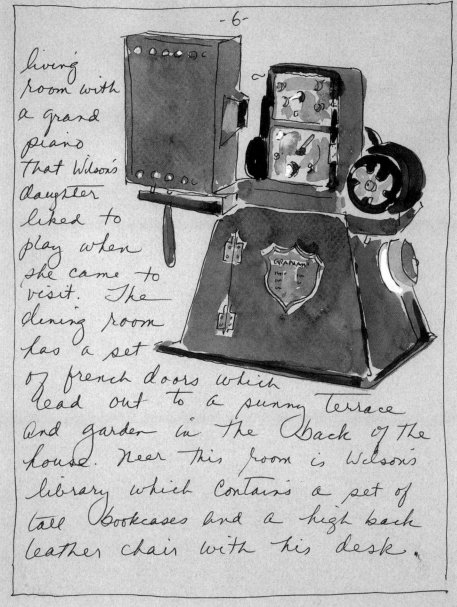

living room with a grand piano that Wilson's daughter liked to play when she came to visit. The dining room has a set of french doors which lead out to a sunny terrace and garden in the back of the house. Near this room is Wilson's library which contains a set of tall bookcases and a high back leather chair with his desk.

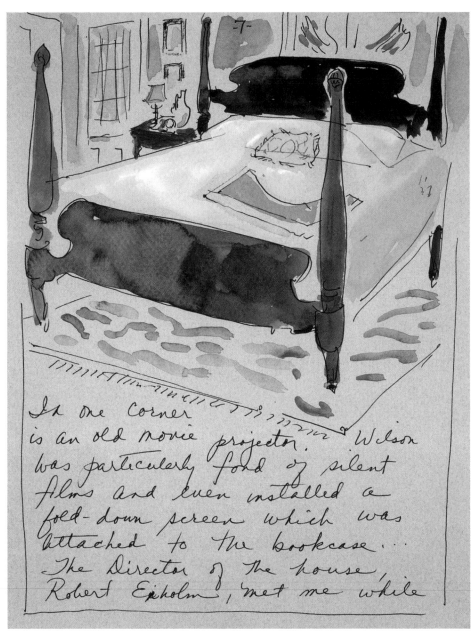

In one corner
is an old movie projector. Wilson
was particularly fond of silent
films and even installed a
fold-down screen which was
attached to the bookcase...
The Director of the house,
Robert Enkholm, met me while

I was sketching some interiors
and showed me an old microphone
that Wilson used to give some
radio addresses. Enkholm is a
font of information and spoke to
me at length about Wilson's

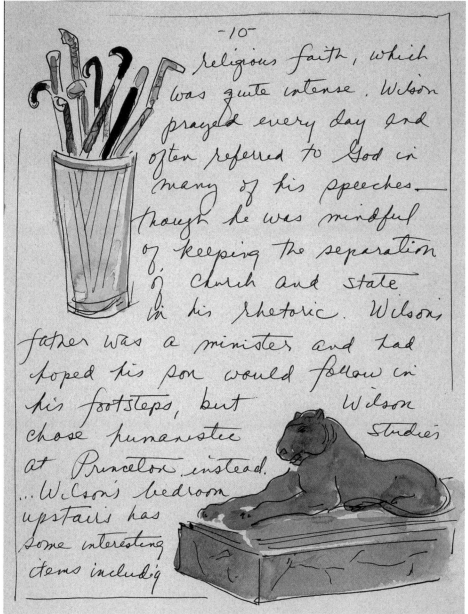

religious faith, which was quite intense. Wilson prayed every day and often referred to God in many of his speeches. Though he was mindful of keeping the separation of church and state in his rhetoric. Wilson's father was a minister and had hoped his son would follow in his footsteps, but Wilson chose humanistic studies at Princeton instead. ...Wilson's bedroom upstairs has some interesting items including

-11-

a set of canes he used in his
last years. He was quite frail
during the period he lived here
and it was quite an effort to
travel, so he preferred to receive
guests at his house... Before
heading back to NYC, I bought

-12-

The new biography
of Wilson by A. Scott
Berg, which is very
good, but long...
I send my best wishes to you
and Rosalee, Adam

JOHN F. KENNEDY HOUSE, BROOKLINE, MA

JOE AND ROSE KENNEDY HOME, HYANNIS PORT, MA

JOHN F. KENNEDY (1917-1963)

[term: 1961-1963]

WHEN I FIRST TRIED to find John F. Kennedy's birthplace in Brookline, Massachusetts, I walked right past it. The three-story house is not very large, and it sits on a small lot like most of its neighbors. But 83 Beals Street is not without its charms; and though JFK only lived there a few years, the house is worth a visit.

The entrance has a homey front porch, a small stoop and a stone marker bearing a bas-relief of JFK's profile. The National Park Service bought the house in 1969, fifty years after the Kennedys originally sold it, and invited Rose Kennedy to "come home" to re-create the rooms just as she remembered them. She joined forces with her longtime decorator Robert Luddington, of the famed department store Jordan Marsh, and completely overhauled the interiors, even finding and repossessing some of the original furnishings.

The dining room, which I saw first, looks like a museum to do-mestic bliss: the table is perfectly set with linens and the family's original china and silverware, suggesting a sumptuous meal about to be served. I could almost smell the clam chowder, a favorite of Jack's since childhood, and Boston cream pie, which Rose loved to make.

My tour guide, ranger Jim Roberts, pointed out the framed reproductions of Renaissance masters in each room. They were meant to inspire and uplift the children, priming them for great things. In the master bedroom, I observed figurines of the crucifix and the Virgin Mary above the beds. Both Joe and Rose were devout Catholics. Family photographs line the stair landing, including one of JFK as a quarterback in prep school. I was shown a set of small notecards in Rose's desk where she kept detailed records, written in her precise script, of every important date in her children's medical history. As a toddler, Jack was diagnosed with Addison's disease, which contributed to his chronic back pain later in life.

Roberts then suggested I walk a few blocks to a larger house on Abbotsford Road, where Joe moved his growing family after he became head of the Columbia Trust Bank. Their new residence was much grander, with a wraparound porch, handsome turrets, and a bigger yard. Since the property is privately owned, I didn't go in, but painted it from the sidewalk across the street.

Both these houses were informative, but they only represent a brief period in JFK's childhood. It would require a trip to Hyannis Port to learn about the further origins of the president with whom the nation would fall in love.

The home on the Cape continues to be privately owned by the Kennedys, and to gain access to it requires special permission. My contact, Jim Shea of the Edward M. Kennedy Institute, kindly met me there shortly after Thanksgiving to give me a private tour. I was introduced to Maureen Lowney, who helps manage the estate, and "Artie," who has been the caretaker since the 1970s. My first stop was Shea's iPhone. He showed me a photo, taken the day before, of the Kennedys playing their annual touch football game on the front lawn—still keeping up tradition after all these years.

I was next shown JFK's bedroom, untouched since he died, with the same chest of drawers, rugs, curtains, and framed prints. In the "den" nearby, photographs from the Kennedys' years in London, when Joe was ambassador, are neatly arranged in a montage on the wall. By the piano, where Rose held forth on summer afternoons, there is a touching letter, framed, of young Teddy telling his father how proud he was of his new bike.

In the attic, I saw a host of Kennedy memorabilia, including stacks of books, a television from the 1950s, Rose's wheelchair, and piles of carefully rolled carpets and curtains from various rooms in the house, each cataloged like sacred artifacts.

The basement offered more discoveries: a home theater and projector Joe had installed in the 1920s to show first-run movies from Hollywood. The patriarch had made a fortune investing in "talkies" against everyone's advice.

Once outside, I painted a picture of the façade of the house, with its three large gables and array of porches and sunlit windows. My back was to the sea, but I turned often to view the beach and waves, which must have provided a happy constant in the turbulent, legendary, and ultimately tragic life of our thirty-fifth president.

It was thrilling to visit the home of a family so much a part of America's heritage. I felt fortunate to have entered this private world, which few have had the privilege to experience, made even more interesting by the fact that the items in the house were not "curated": the family photos, paintings, and books were all where the Kennedys would have left them.

My only previous encounter with the Kennedy family was over forty years ago, in the summer of 1969, when I visited Robert Kennedy's home with my parents. Hickory Hill in McClean, Virginia, had been previously owned by JFK but was then sold to Bobby in 1961. Arrangements for our visit were made for us through the writer Richard Goodwin—a speechwriter for JFK—and his wife, the historian Doris Kearns Goodwin, who had been renting our house in Cambridge. I distinctly recall arriving at the large white colonial and being greeted at the door by a young Caroline Kennedy, then about my age. She said hello and then, either out of shyness or indifference, promptly darted back upstairs to her room. I remember a pool house covered top to bottom with family snapshots. The signature Kennedy grin was everywhere, at beaches on the Cape, on the tennis court, on sailboats.

Looking back on my experience at Hyannis Port, I reflected on JFK the president. Like most Americans, I am inordinately familiar with stories from the legend of Camelot. Kennedy's career emerged with the advent of television, and the debate between him and Nixon was decided by sweaty brows rather than substantive issues. But who was JFK, *really*? Merely a glamorous face successfully steered into politics by a Machiavellian father? Seeing the house where JFK lived left me eager to learn more. Back in New York I bought a copy of Ted Sorensen's biography. The author, who had also been one of JFK's speechwriters, describes him as an extremely well read, thoughtful, and compassionate man who was deeply affected by the plight of the less fortunate. Sorensen details one episode when they both visited a coal mine in West Virginia, and JFK was so moved by the poverty he saw that the president could barely speak. Jack was very much his own man, and though he welcomed the support of his father, he was not compelled to change his political views to placate him. It seems that these strong family bonds, so evident in JFK's intimate connection to his homes in Brookline and Hyannis Port, formed the character of a great mind and great man.

ADAM VAN DOREN
130 WEST 57TH STREET · 13-B
NEW YORK, NEW YORK 10019

November, 12, 2013

51 Abbottsford Rd
Brookline, MA

Dear David,
It was truly a memorable night in Stockbridge last week. Henry, Charlotte and I were so pleased to be included

83 Beals Street

at your dinner table honoring Wendell
Minor at the Red Lion Inn. I
very much enjoyed hearing about
your experience meeting Norman
Rockwell over fifty years ago. As
a recent college graduate, you must

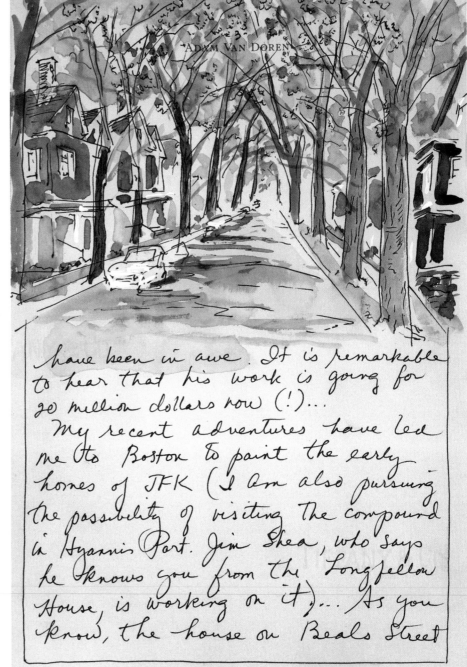

have been in awe. It is remarkable
to hear that his work is going for
20 million dollars now (!)...
My recent adventures have led
me to Boston to paint the early
homes of JFK (I am also pursuing
the possibility of visiting the compound
in Hyannis Port. Jim Shea, who says
he knows you from the Longfellow
House, is working on it)... As you
know, the house on Beals Street

in Brookline is
where the President
lived for the first four years
of his life. Then, as Joe's family
grew, they moved a few blocks
away to a bigger house on
Abbotsford Road. The latter home
is now privately owned, but I
managed to set up my stool
across the street to do the

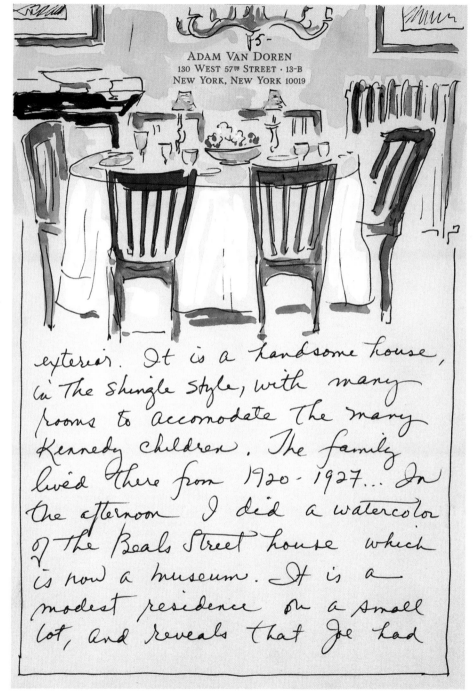

exterior. It is a handsome house,
in The Shingle Style, with many
rooms to accomodate the many
Kennedy children. The family
lived there from 1920 - 1927... In
the afternoon I did a watercolor
of the Beals Street house which
is now a museum. It is a
modest residence on a small
lot, and reveals that Joe had

not quite amassed his substantial fortune yet. In the front of the house on this nicely tree-lined street is an historic marker with a bas-relief of JFK. I was able to meet with Jim Roberts, a curator, who

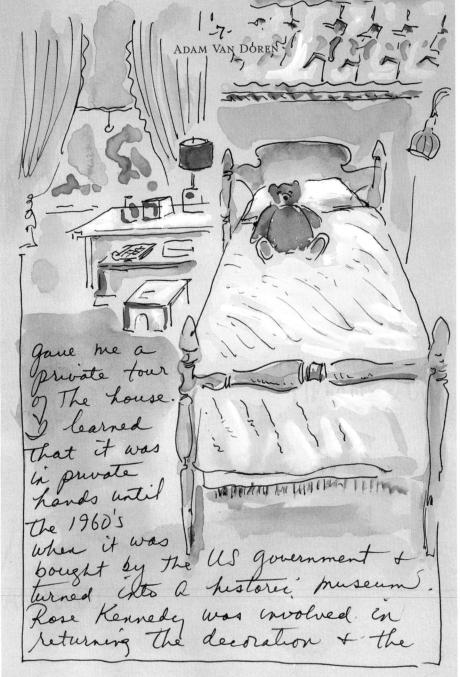

gave me a private tour of the house. I learned that it was in private hands until the 1960's when it was bought by the US government & turned into a historic museum. Rose Kennedy was involved in returning the decoration & the

furniture to
the way it was when she lived
in it during the early 1900s. The
old wallpaper, paint colors, etc. were
recreated to be as authentic.
as possible ... In the dining
room I noticed a small

miniature version of the main
table, with two little chairs and
small silver bowls. Apparently it
was meant for JFK and his
brother Joe. They were not allowed
to join the main table till they
were seven, but in the

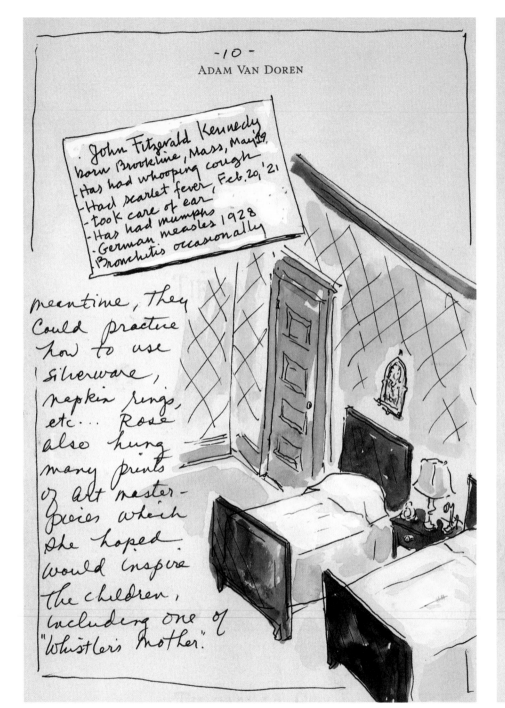

· John Fitzgerald Kennedy
born Brookline, Mass, May 29.
- Has had whooping cough
- Had scarlet fever, Feb. 20, '21
- took care of ear
- Has had mumps
- German measles 1928
- Bronchitis occasionally

meantime, they could practice how to use silverware, napkin rings, etc... Rose also hung many prints of art master-pieces which she hoped would inspire the children, including one of "Whistler's Mother."

The master bedroom has two separate beds with Catholic icons hanging over each headboard.
In addition to being quite religious, Rose was extremely organized. She kept detailed records of each child's medical history, neatly recorded on 4 x 6 note cards. Rose was from

JFK, age 3

a substantial family, the Fitzgeralds, and I believe her father had been mayor of Boston. He thought she was marrying "down" when she got engaged to Joe.... Before

heading back to New York, I
bought a biography of JFK to
read with me on the train.
There are thousands to choose
from, but I thought I would
get Ted Sorensen's, since Ted had
had such an intimate connection
with Kennedy as his speechwriter.
I was impressed with how
Sorensen depicted Kennedy as a

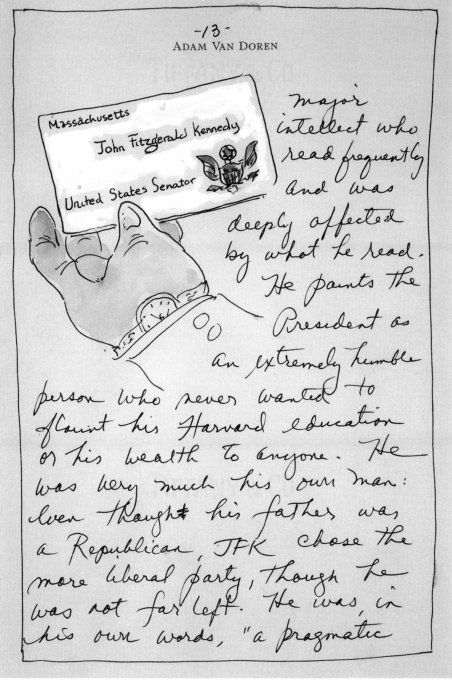

major
intellect who
read frequently
and was
deeply affected
by what he read.
He paints the
President as
an extremely humble
person who never wanted to
flaunt his Harvard education
or his wealth to anyone. He
was very much his own man:
even though his father was
a Republican, JFK chose the
more liberal party, though he
was not far left. He was, in
his own words, "a pragmatic

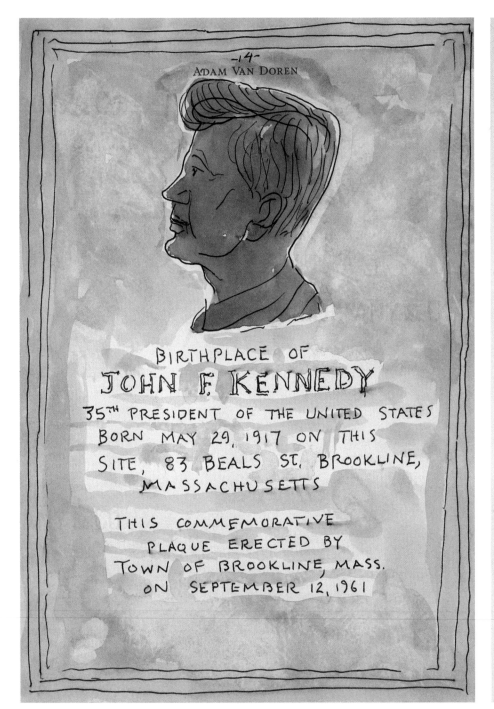

BIRTHPLACE OF
JOHN F. KENNEDY
35TH PRESIDENT OF THE UNITED STATES
BORN MAY 29, 1917 ON THIS
SITE, 83 BEALS ST. BROOKLINE,
MASSACHUSETTS

THIS COMMEMORATIVE
PLAQUE ERECTED BY
TOWN OF BROOKLINE, MASS.
ON SEPTEMBER 12, 1961

He has served ALL Massachusetts with Distinction!

RE-ELECT U.S. SENATOR KENNEDY

"A PROFILE IN COURAGE"

ELECT U.S. SENATOR JOHN F. KENNEDY VICE PRESIDENT

KENNEDY FOR PRESIDENT

KENNEDY FOR PRESIDENT

liberal, a pratical liberal." He
was also aware of how much
privilege he was born with, and
how much help he had received
from others along the way. He
wrote: "A hundred times a day
I remind myself that my inner
and outer life depend on the

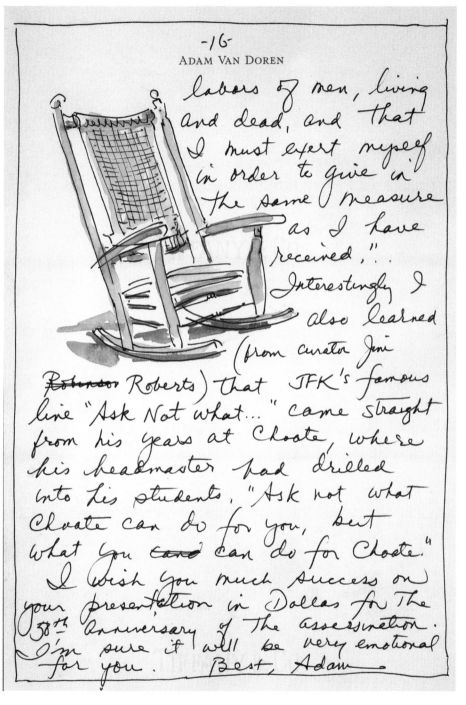

labors of men, living
and dead, and that
I must exert myself
in order to give in
the same measure
as I have
received,"...
Interestingly I
also learned
(from curator Jim
~~Robinson~~ Roberts) that JFK's ~~famous~~
line "Ask Not what..." came straight
from his years at Choate, where
his headmaster had drilled
into his students, "Ask not what
Choate can do for you, but
what you ~~can~~ can do for Choate."
I wish you much success on
your presentation in Dallas for the
50th anniversary of the assassination.
I'm sure it will be very emotional
for you. Best, Adam

P.S. If possible, I would also be
~~interested~~ interested in
your suggestion of
Bush's ranch when I
to visit LBJ's site...
P.P.S. All my best to
Rosalee

pursuing
painting
go

Campaigning
in Logan County,
West Virginia

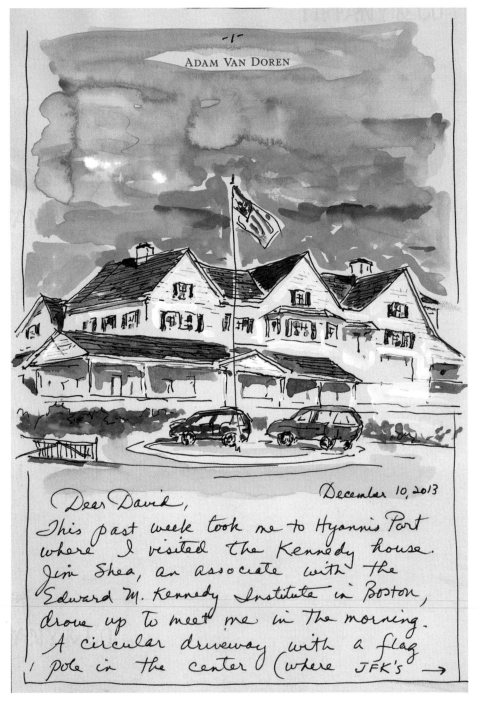

December 10, 2013

Dear David,

This past week took me to Hyannis Port where I visited the Kennedy house. Jim Shea, an associate with the Edward M. Kennedy Institute in Boston, drove up to meet me in the morning. A circular driveway with a flag pole in the center (where JFK's →

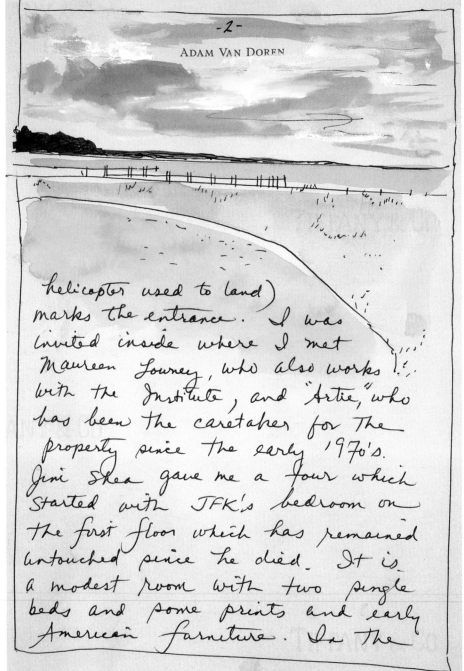

helicopter used to land) marks the entrance. I was invited inside where I met Maureen Lowney, who also works with the Institute, and "Artie," who has been the caretaker for the property since the early 1970's. Jim Shea gave me a tour which started with JFK's bedroom on the first floor which has remained untouched since he died. It is a modest room with two single beds and some prints and early American furniture. In the

sitting *room* off JFK's bedroom there was
an elevator installed for Joe Kennedy
after he had a severe stroke. The
room looks very "lived-in" with many
photos on the wall of the family.
Jim showed me a copy of one of

Rose's books from the bookcase. It
was Arthur Schlesinger's biography of
JFK in which she had pencil notes
in the margins throughout. She was
meticulous about "correcting" the

ADAM VAN DOREN

facts from the historical accounts she had thought Schlesinger had gotten wrong. On one wall was an extensive array of family photos of the Kennedy's time in England when he was the Ambassador. ... In The main living room is a grand piano which Rose used to play every afternoon during the summer. The family was encouraged to gather around for sing-a-longs which she orchestrated. The dining room beyond the foyer is where the Kennedys — to this

day - apparently still dress for dinner. It seems that Teddy was the last family member to use the house on a regular basis. His home office still has his papers on his desk... Jim then took me on a tour of the attic where I saw

JFK and Joe Kennedy
c. 1961

A number of interesting things including Rose's wheelchair and the family's original television set from the 1950's. A number of clothes were hanging in closets along with rugs that were wrapped & clearly labeled from which rooms they came from.

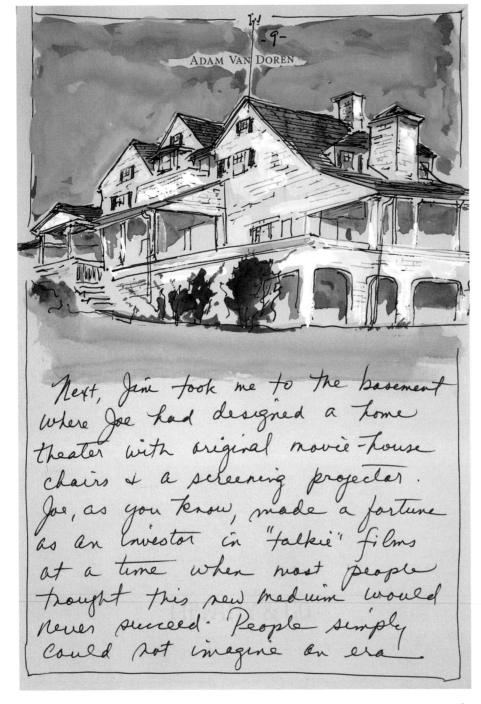

Next, Jim took me to the basement where Joe had designed a home theater with original movie-house chairs & a screening projector. Joe, as you know, made a fortune as an investor in "talkie" films at a time when most people thought this new medium would never succeed. People simply could not imagine an era

after silent movies. After the tour, I went outside to paint on The Lawn. In keeping with family tradition, The Kennedy Cousins' had gathered for a touch-football game the day before. As I was about to leave at the end of The day, I had the pleasure of meeting Ted Kennedy's two Portugese water dogs, "Cappy" & "Sonny", who came to visit. "Cappy", named for Captains Courageous, is the brother of Obama's dog "Bo"...

ADAM VAN DOREN

Both dogs are quite large and apparently have insatiable appetites. They had both just gotten back from the hospital because they had eaten raisins, which can kill a dog... Driving back from the house to New York, I realized I had had a "remarkable experience" seeing a President's home before it has become a museum ... As discussed, I am more than happy to have you extend the deadline of your preface till the beginning of March ... In the mean time, best to you & Rosalee—
Adam

WHEATLAND, LANCASTER, PENNSYLVANIA

JAMES BUCHANAN (1791–1868)

[*term: 1857–1861*]

I WAS MET AT THE FRONT DOOR of Wheatland by curator Patrick Clarke, whom I'd made arrangements to meet the week before. No sooner had we shaken hands than he broadsided me: "Buchanan, you know, is generally recognized as our *worst* president." I admit I was taken aback by such an emphatically critical remark, but at the same time I appreciated his off-the-cuff candor. I confessed I had not known this fact, or much else about our fifteenth president. But that was the reason I'd come: I wanted to learn more. I wanted, I admit, to *like* Buchanan.

Clarke, undeterred, continued, "Buchanan's greatest fault was the slavery issue; he basically kicked the can down the road and dropped it on Lincoln's lap." Playing the apologist, I now hopefully pleaded, "Didn't Buchanan have any *positive* qualities?" "Well . . ." said Clarke. "He proudly served his country as Secretary of State, U.S. senator, member of the House, and ambassador to Russia." Now things were looking up; that roll-call of respectable public service sounded none too shabby, especially for such a mysteriously marginalized president. After all, a robust fifteen thousand

people still visit his home annually, so perhaps a Buchanan comeback is finally in the offing.

Wheatland is a solid brick Federal with white trim and green shutters, set well back from the road in the midst of a serviceable, if somewhat lackluster, landscape. Vestiges of a once-greater estate abound and can be seen in the majestic old-growth trees that surround the house. Only ten acres remain of the original stately twenty-two. At the rear of the dwelling I found a spot next to a quaint old smokehouse, set up my paints and brushes, and began to work. Starting to draw the outline of the roof with my pencil, I soon noticed how uncharacteristically elongated the house was and how disproportionately shallow its sides were. Two gangling, enervated three-story wings flanked the house's central section. The effect is presumptuously outstretched and flattened. Wheatland, it dawned upon me, was all about the façade; it was deliberately designed to appear grander than it actually was. Was this house, I wondered, a metaphor for Buchanan himself?

Touring the inside of the home, I was disappointed to discover that much of the furniture consisted of replicas. There are, however, some fine rooms with high ceilings, ornate moldings, and handsome marble fireplaces. A number of personal items still remain, mostly consisting of Buchanan's books and copious papers. It was interesting to see the desk in his study, with its original pen and inkwell. Looking at a book on the shelf, I discovered an account of the president by James Gordon Bennett from 1856. "Mr. Buchanan—called 'Jeems Buck-an-an' by Southern gentlemen, and 'Jimmy Bewchanan' by his old townsmen . . . sits in his high-back chair, beside the open door. He wears a loose gown made of checkered calico, not at all Romanesque or picturesque in its effect. He has light slippers on his feet and a cigar in his mouth, and is evidently going for comfort."

Great pains have been made by the Lancaster Historical Society (which now manages the home) to match the original wallpaper, draperies, and floor coverings. I was generously given permission to paint in one of the parlors, and I focused on rendering its most impressive features: a gilded recherché mirror over the mantelpiece, a voluminous Victorian bookcase, and an intricately carved grand piano.

Upstairs, the high-ceilinged rooms continued, mostly comprised of bedrooms for the nieces and nephews. Buchanan was, notably, our only bachelor president. A state-of-the-art bathtub, replete with metal lining and chrome fixtures, seemed what it was once was—the height of luxury. It was especially desirable when one considers what sanitation meant for the average person in the middle 1800s: a toilet was literally a hole in the ground, or, if you were lucky, an outhouse that supported your derriere with barn board and rusty nails. Consider the splinters.

The kitchen space in the basement looked primitive to me, but, in fact, was fairly plush for Buchanan's day and well equipped with iron pans and copper pots. Buchanan was quite the epicurean, and given his proclivity for lavish White House dinners, the president and his guests most certainly enjoyed sumptuous food at Wheatland. He is known, for instance, to have had fresh butter sent from Philadelphia in locked brassbound kettles, and he was particularly fond of German sauerkraut and Pennsylvania Dutch recipes such as stuffed shoulder of pork, gooseberry tarts, sauerbraten, and cinnamon apples.

As I strolled through the corridors, I sensed this was the house of an unflappably self-assured man, proud of himself and of his Lancaster connections (he moved to the city in 1809 to study law). Lancaster, after all, was then Pennsylvania's most prosperous inland city and once the state capital. This particular city father was, to all appearances, superciliously aware of where he stood—and not shy at all about asserting his rightful pride of place. Judging from his marble bust and haughty half-length portrait, Buchanan was nothing if not vain about his looks: in each rendering, he sports a raffishly upturned shock of white hair just above his forehead—no doubt the latest in men's style at the time—but a little too foppishly just so. Perhaps such vainglory and desire to be fashionable was also his weakness, a man who so liked being liked (over ten thousand people attended his funeral, in 1868) that he complacently ignored the untenable nature of the status quo. Playing it safe—allowing the states to decide slavery for themselves, in lieu of confronting, inconveniently, the impending issues of secession and a possible civil war—gave him a chance to retire in peace and live out his life quietly in the city he had grown to love. In fairness to Buchanan, he was saddled with a contentious Congress, not unlike what Obama faces today, which was unwilling to allow military force to curb insurrections in the South. It would take Fort Sumter, six weeks into Lincoln's term, to force the issue.

"If you are as happy entering the White House," he revealingly told Lincoln, "as I shall feel on returning to Wheatland, you are a happy man indeed."

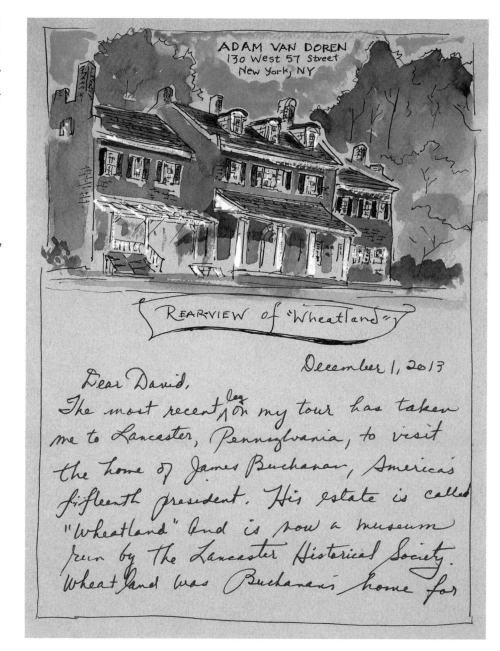

ADAM VAN DOREN
130 West 57 Street
New York, NY

REAR-VIEW of "Wheatland"

December 1, 2013

Dear David,
The most recent leg on my tour has taken me to Lancaster, Pennsylvania, to visit the home of James Buchanan, America's fifteenth president. His estate is called "Wheatland" and is now a museum run by the Lancaster Historical Society. Wheatland was Buchanan's home for

- 2 -

many years, especially later in life.
He is the only president not to be married,
but ~~his~~ he shared his home with
his niece Harriet Lane... I arrived to
Lancaster by train (the city has an
impressive railway station) and met the

THE SIGNATURE OF JAMES BUCHANAN...

James Buchanan

- 3 -

Curator Patrick
house site.
Considerable
and was
saying that
considered
to be

Clarke at the
Clarke knows a
amount of history
not shy about
Buchanan is
by many historians
among our

James Buchanan
15th President

least distinguished
presidents.
Buchanan is
known for being
soft on the slavery
issue, and for
essentially leaving
it to Abraham
Lincoln to find a
solution. Although Buchanan
recognized the moral evils of slavery,
he defended states'
rights which empower'd
the South. This
~~duplicity~~ ~~ambivalence~~ ultimately
created a more fractious
country rather than
a more unified one
which Buchanan
had hoped to
create. Though Buchanan

SMOKEHOUSE

was by no means the only president
to essentially appease the South
on the   slavery issue
(his four   predecessors did
roughly   the same thing)
~~but~~ he   is criticized
the most   because the
most   glaring
warning   signs of
an   impending
war   occurred
during   his tenure:
the   Dred Scott

Harriet Lane, niece of
James Buchanan

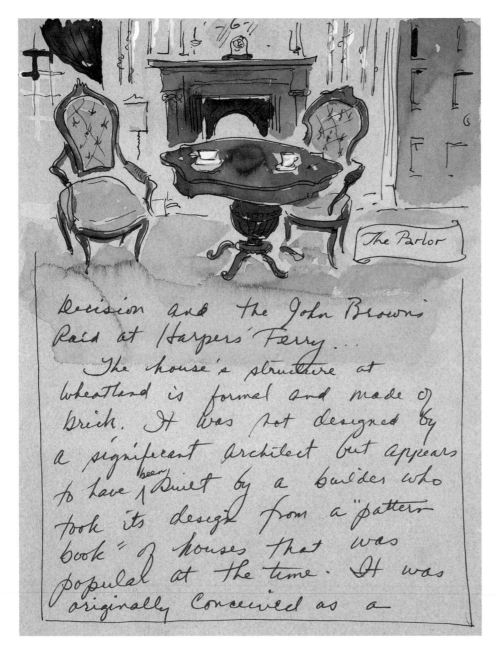

The Parlor

decision and the John Brown's
Raid at Harpers' Ferry...

The house's structure at
Wheatland is formal and made of
brick. It was not designed by
a significant Architect but appears
to have been Built by a builder who
took its design from a "pattern
book" of houses that was
popular at the time. It was
originally conceived as a

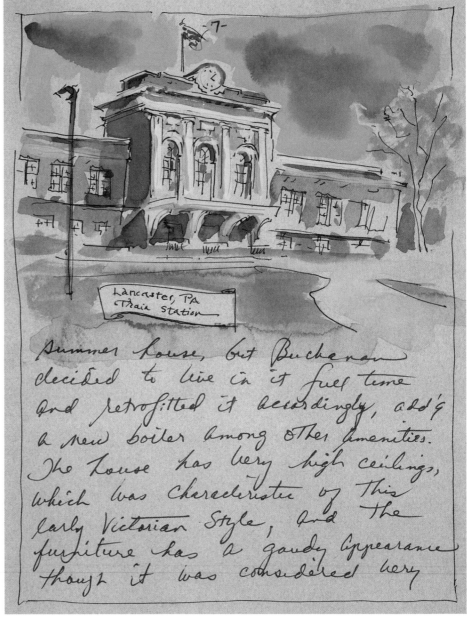

Lancaster, PA
Train Station

summer house, but Buchanan
decided to live in it full time
and retrofitted it accordingly, add'g
a new boiler among other amenities.
The house has very high ceilings,
which was characteristic of this
early Victorian Style, and the
furniture has a gaudy appearance
though it was considered very

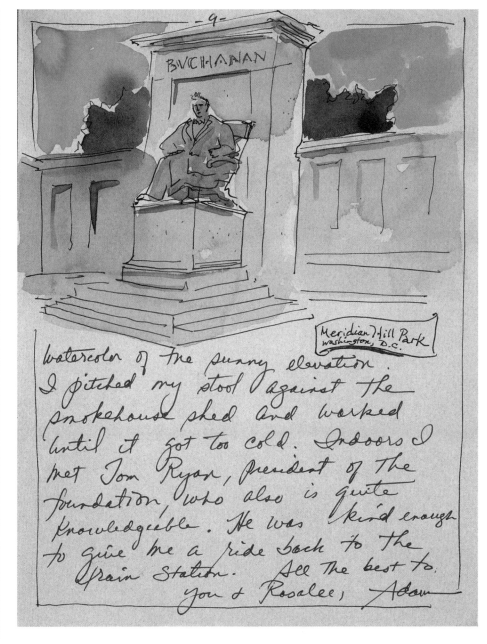

-8-

A PUBLIC MEETING — WILL BE HELD — THURSDAY EVENING DRED SCOTT CASE

Contemporary for its day. About 70 per cent of the artifacts in the house are connected with Buchanan, according to curator Clarke. A marble bust of the president has the characteristic stand of hair on the forehead which was popular in the 1850's. The house is set back on a large lawn and is notable for a grand entrance porch with several steps. I walked to the back of the house to do a

-9-

BUCHANAN

Meridian Hill Park washington, D.C.

watercolor of the sunny elevation. I pitched my stool against the smokehouse shed and worked until it got too cold. Indoors I met Tom Ryan, president of the foundation, who also is quite knowledgeable. He was kind enough to give me a ride back to the train station. All the best to you & Rosalee, Adam

CALVIN COOLIDGE HISTORIC SITE, PLYMOUTH NOTCH, VERMONT

CALVIN COOLIDGE (1872-1933)

[term of office: 1923-1929]

IN THE DEAD OF WINTER, with fourteen inches of snow on the ground, the Calvin Coolidge homestead in Plymouth Notch, Vermont, was honestly not high on my list of presidential homes to visit. After all, "Silent Cal" is not considered our most colorful president, nor our most distinguished. Dorothy Parker famously quipped after he died, "How could they tell?" But I wanted to give Coolidge the benefit of the doubt; there had to be more to the man. Shortly after Christmas then, I persuaded my teenage son Henry, a history buff, to join me on the five-hour trek up Route 91 from our house in Cornwall, Connecticut. We arrived as the sun was going down on the tiny village, blanketed in twilight winter white like a Currier and Ives print. As picturesque as it looked, the location must have been intensely isolating in Coolidge's time. Today we romanticize these quaint corners of the world, because within them we can be free from urban sprawl and still feel connected by phone, Internet, FedEx, four-wheel drive. But in 1900, if you had an emergency that required medical attention and needed to get to the nearest big town, you were as good as dead. Self-preservation and self-sufficiency went hand in hand if you wanted to live past forty.

We were met in Plymouth by the local curator William Jenney, who led us on a tour of the Coolidge sites. They comprise three-fourths of the town. Our first stop was the modest eighteenth-century clapboard house where Calvin Coolidge was born. It was attached to the back of the country store where his father worked. Calvin's boyhood room, which was barely large enough to fit his bed, felt like an icebox. "This is nothing," Jenney said, referring to the frigid temperature outside. "It could get to thirty below some winters, and there was no heat except a kitchen stove." Other stops included a larger house across the street, where the family moved in 1881 for more living space. The new house was connected to a barn, typical of these upper New England farmsteads, and Calvin's chores of cleaning the smelly stables, collecting firewood, even knitting blankets, kept him busy all year. The kitchen in the house was as bare as can be, with open shelves and a simple sink, but presumably Coolidge was not deprived, for he remained steadfastly nostalgic for his childhood favorites such as Vermont country pickles, pork apple pie, and cornmeal muffins.

We next visited the parlor room, immortalized in a painting by

Arthur Keller, where Coolidge, the then-vice president was sworn into office upon hearing the news that President Warren G. Harding had died. Calvin's father Edward, as a justice of the peace, had presided over the ceremony. I took a photograph of Henry standing where Coolidge had stood. Despite lacking a few extra inches and thinning hair, my son looked every bit the part. The furniture has been preserved, and is simple and sparse, reminiscent of these austere, hardboiled Yankees themselves. Social life in Plymouth in those years must have been limited to a few neighbors, family members—and perhaps livestock? Given his stark upbringing and surroundings, it is perhaps no wonder Calvin was a man of few words; he spent his hours observing, reading, and reflecting. A man of principle, frugality, and "transparency" (remarkably, he held more press conferences than any president up to that time), the one element Calvin Coolidge seemed to lack was charisma.

Coolidge, overshadowed perhaps by the Roaring Twenties (who could compete with that?) and Charles Lindbergh's heroics, did not leave many memorable impressions on the country when he retired from office. His wife Grace appears to have been a bigger hit. But Coolidge, also, seems not to have left the country in any worse shape than when he arrived at the White House, in 1923. We neither engaged in war nor suffered any major economic downturns, and Coolidge's corruption-free administration was a welcome respite after the Teapot Dome scandal during Harding's tenure. I concluded that even quiet and contemplative men often have considerable talents for leadership.

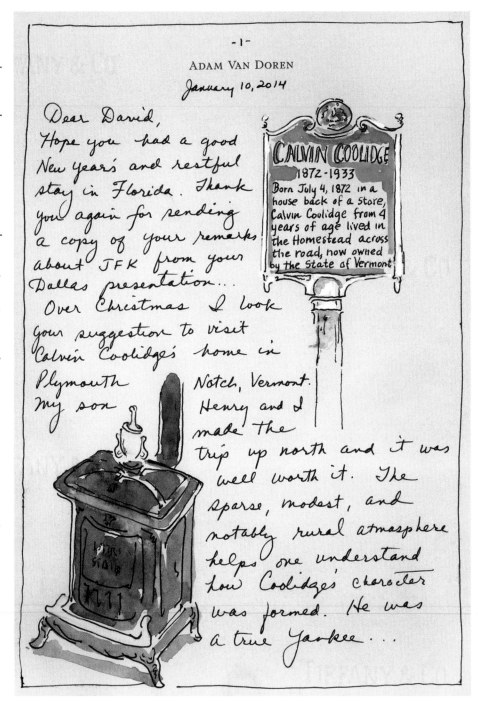

Blanketed under fourteen inches of snow, the little village where Coolidge was born has been left untouched since he died. A number of structures in the town, which is tiny, have some relation to the Coolidge family. In fact, some descendants

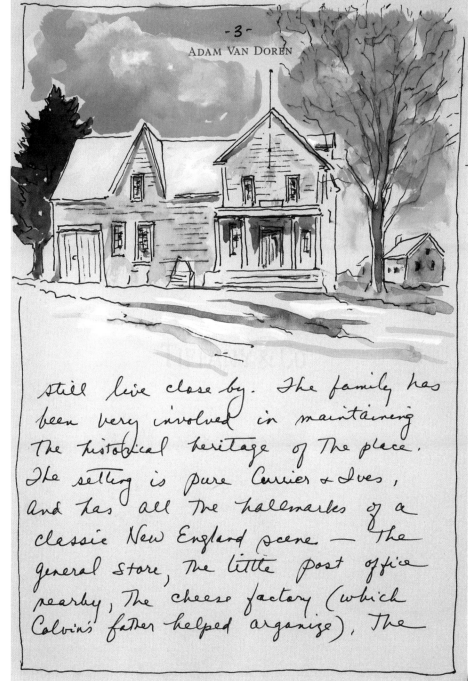

still live close by. The family has been very involved in maintaining the historical heritage of the place. The setting is pure Currier & Ives, and has all the hallmarks of a classic New England scene — the general store, the little post office nearby, the cheese factory (which Calvin's father helped organize). The

White Colonial meeting a house, all nestled among the snowy green mountains. The Coolidge sites are maintained by The Vermont Historical Society and were closed for the season, but Henry and I were given a private tour by William Jenney, one of the curators. He took us first to Calvin's birthplace, a small wooden structure that

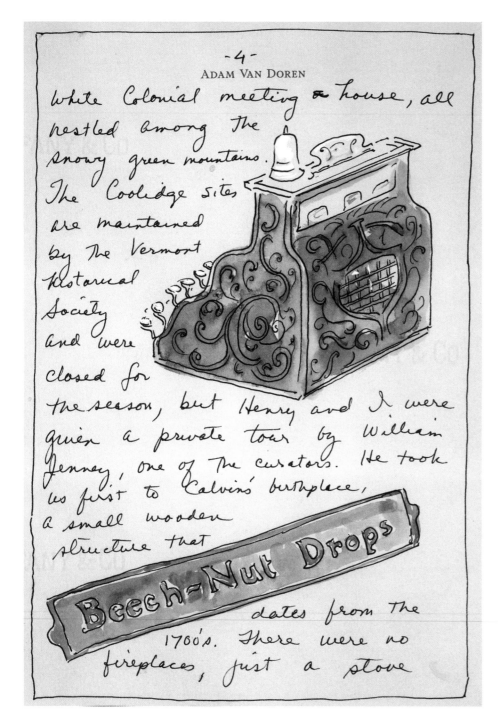

dates from the 1700's. There were no fireplaces, just a stove

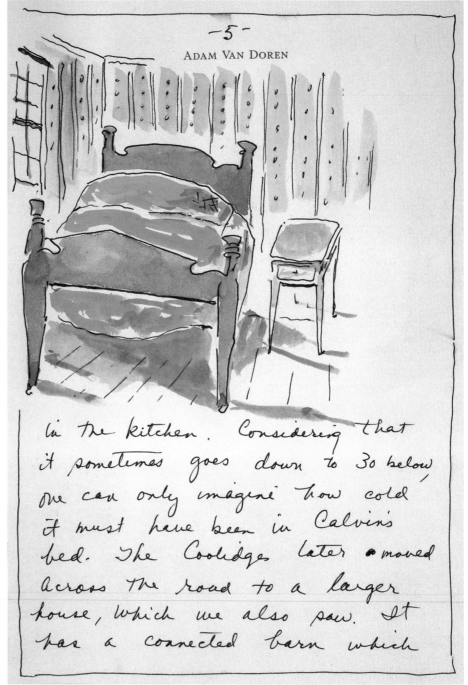

in the kitchen. Considering that it sometimes goes down to 30 below, one can only imagine how cold it must have been in Calvin's bed. The Coolidges later a moved across the road to a larger house, which we also saw. It has a connected barn which

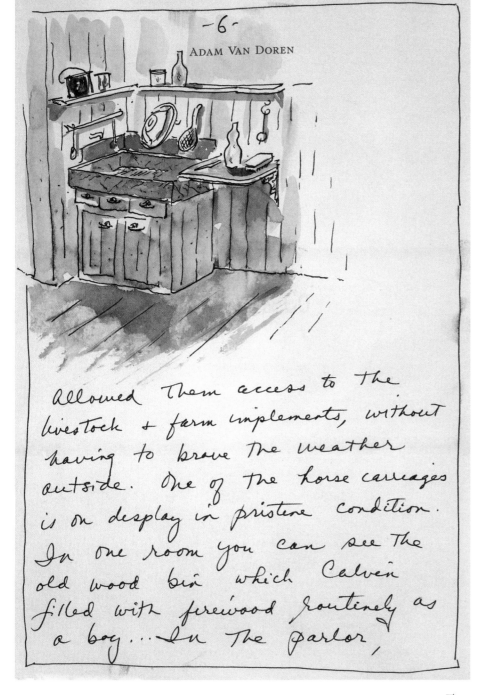

Allowed them access to the livestock & farm implements, without having to brave the weather outside. One of the horse carriages is on display in pristine condition. In one room you can see the old wood bin which Calvin filled with firewood routinely as a boy.... In the parlor,

Henry and I stood where Calvin was given the oath of office as president when Harding died in office in the middle of his term. Calvin's father did the honors because he was a justice of the peace in town. The scene was not photographed, but a painter Arthur Keller

immortalized it by positioning the figures just as Coolidge remembered them. To this day, the

Kerosene lamp and round table are situated just as they were those many years ago. It is straight out of Norman Rockwell,

And has been a favorite stop for tourists for decades. At one point, as many as 15,000 people descended on Plymouth over a course of a summer in the 1920's just to get a glimpse of the famous parlor. Coolidge described

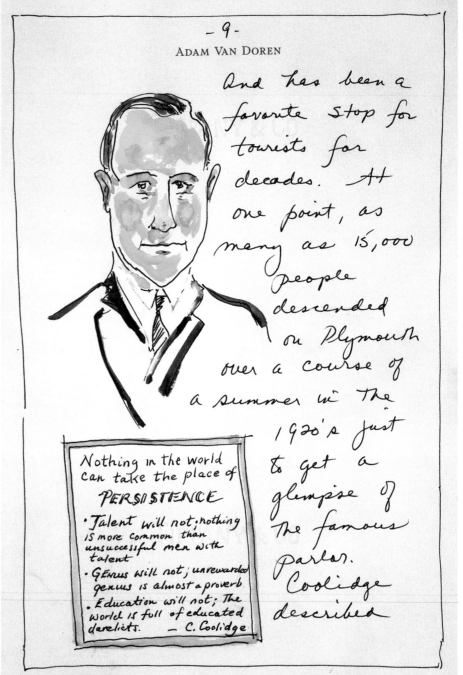

Nothing in the world can take the place of
PERSISTENCE
• Talent will not; nothing is more common than unsuccessful men with talent
• Genius will not; unrewarded genius is almost a proverb
• Education will not; The world is full of educated derelicts.
— C. Coolidge

The whole episode in his
autobiography, which critics
have praised as one of the
best presidential memoirs....
Interestingly, for all the

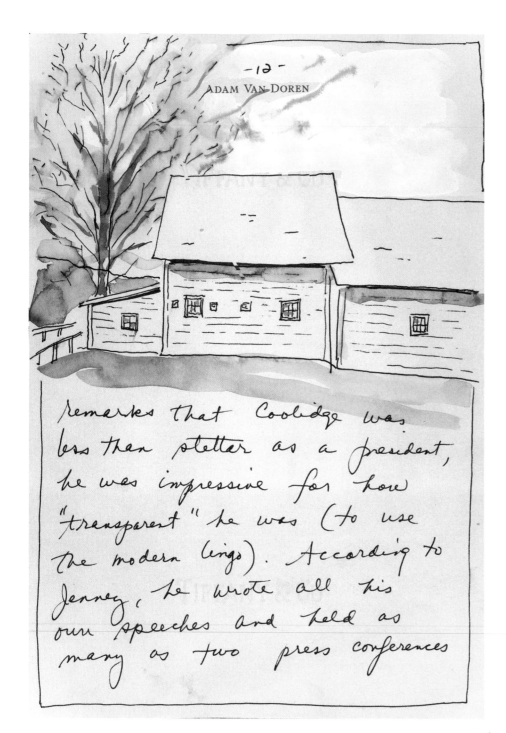

remarks that Coolidge was less than stellar as a president, he was impressive for how "transparent" he was (to use the modern lingo). According to Jenney, he wrote all his own speeches and held as many as two press conferences

a week, more than any other president... An impressive museum display is also available to visit just beyond the general store. It features film footage of Coolidge meeting with American Indians, and it has many artifacts including the hat he wore as a student at Amherst.

Coolidge as a young undergraduate at Amherst

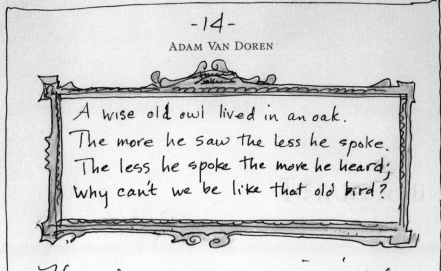

A wise old owl lived in an oak.
The more he saw the less he spoke.
The less he spoke the more he heard;
Why can't we be like that old bird?

There is also an intricately carved wooden chair that the head of Hungary gave to him as a diplomatic gift. In addition, There is a sample radio of The era which would have been The same one people# used to listen to Coolidge's addresses.

There is ample information on Grace Coolidge, who was very popular and was quite the "life of The party." One of The reasons Coolidge is portrayed as being so quiet was because he was often compared to his wife.... Grace was very outspoken about

handcuffs for local jail used by Calvin Coolidge's father

Bin for firewood

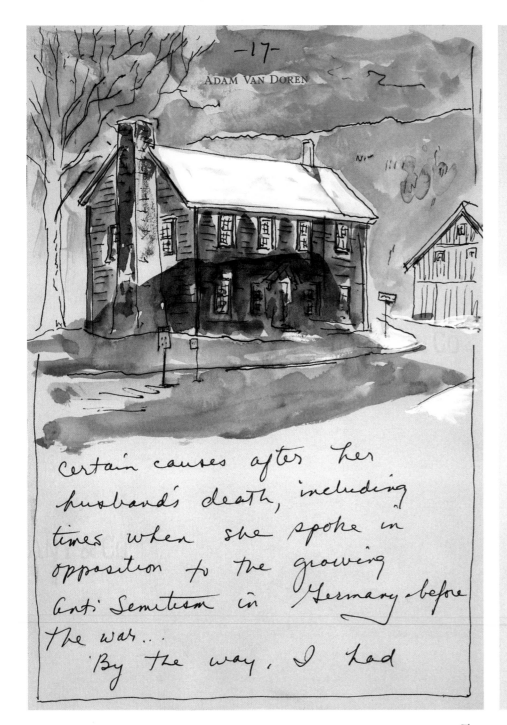

certain causes after her
husband's death, including
times when she spoke in
opposition to the growing
anti-Semitism in Germany before
the war...

By the way, I had

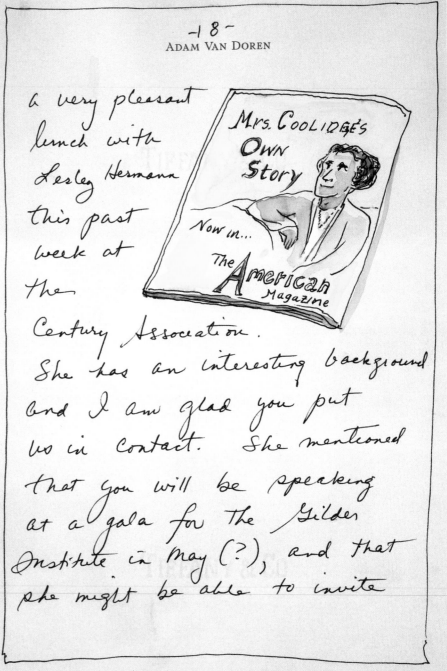

a very pleasant
lunch with
Lesley Hermann
this past
week at
the
Century Association.

She has an interesting background
and I am glad you put
us in contact. She mentioned
that you will be speaking
at a gala for the Gilder
Institute in May (?), and that
she might be able to invite

19

ADAM VAN DOREN

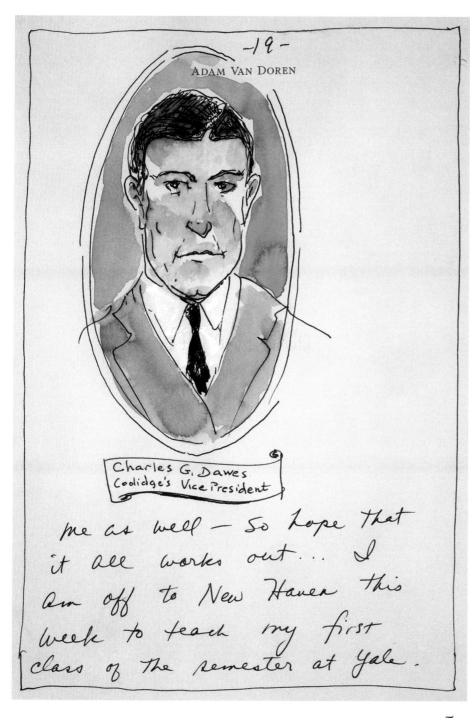

Charles G. Dawes
Coolidge's Vice President

me as well — So hope that
it all works out... I
am off to New Haven this
week to teach my first
class of the semester at Yale.

ADAM VAN DOREN

Over one hundred students signed
up for my seminar, but

COOLIDGE AND A COMMON SENSE

I must
winnow the
number down to 15,..
Hope you're flying
high with the Wright
Brothers, and

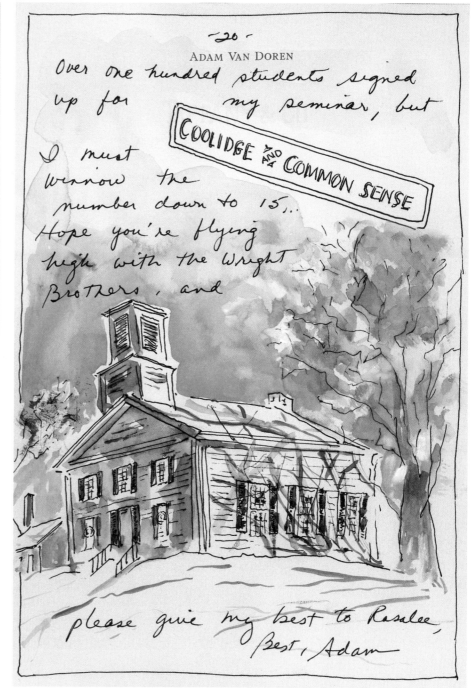

please give my best to Rosalee,
Best, Adam

LINDENWALD, KINDERHOOK, NEW YORK
MARTIN VAN BUREN (1782-1862)

[term of office: 1837-1841]

MARTIN VAN BUREN was known as the "little Magician," given his short stature, but his house Lindenwald stands tall and imposing on the property, crowned with a high lookout tower. A large central gable and ornate entry porch add symmetry. There is little left of any formal gardens; and with the exception of a few majestic trees, the grounds appear uninspired (though I confess my son Henry and I visited it on a dreary day in late fall). The house's Italianate architecture is the latest of several incarnations that transformed Lindenwald from a simple structure to a lavishly grand one. To our disappointment, there is not much remaining of the original furnishings; most are replicas.

Ranger Dawn Roberts was kind enough to allow me to sketch privately in one room, a library that had Gothic bookcases, a marble bust of Van Buren, and a writing desk on loan from the Smithsonian. Since the boiler was turned off for the season, my hands were cold and I drew with my gloves on. The main entrance hall, which Van Buren ingeniously converted into a large dining room, has a mural on four sides with bucolic scenes of a romanticized landscape. I envisioned the leading lights of Kinderhook arriving through the wide Dutch door and feasting on delectable dishes of venison, boar's head, and oysters, Van Buren's favorite.

The high ceilings, however impractical to heat, were the fashion of the day, as was the elaborate switchback staircase with its clumsily designed and overscaled carved balusters. We ascended the steps to the servants' quarters, and Roberts pointed out an old call bell that had just been repaired by a local craftsman. The rooms were bare with peeling stucco, and a musty odor, exacerbated by the damp weather outside, pervaded the house. We then climbed to the tower that affords impressive views of the surrounding area.

When Van Buren looked out across the fields and meadows below (now somewhat spoiled by the Park Service trailers), he must have swelled with pride to own such a mansion in Kinderhook, his birthplace. He was a self-made man who lacked the means to attend college, but was ambitious enough to pass the New York State Bar at twenty-one. As a youth, he had spent hours at his father's tavern, soaking up talk of politicians passing through town. In a nearby section of the local village his Dutch forebears are well represented in the old local graveyard, where Van Buren also rests. Henry and I drove to see it. A tall granite obelisk rises above the president's headstone with its fading inscription. As a light rain was falling, Henry wisely stayed in the car, and I walked around to look at the other graves in the cemetery. Van Alen, Van Alstyne, Van Dyke, Van Santvoord, Van Schaack. The names reminded me that New York City was once called New Amsterdam before the British occupied it.

Van Buren was known for his impressive diplomatic skills, especially in conciliating the other branches of government, and he is credited with helping to form the modern Democratic Party. He was also a distinguished Secretary of State under Andrew Jackson. His extreme loyalty to Jackson made him a part of a political machine that not only got him elected to the presidency, but also won him many favors while in office. Cronyism, not political conviction, was his hallmark. Always the courteous gentleman, he was eager to deflect controversy, and his calmness served him well during the panic of 1837, when the financial bubble—created by Jackson's policies—burst shortly after he assumed power. He effectively fought to disengage the government's finances from the banks, and this strategy is one of his greatest legacies.

Unfortunately, Van Buren's considerable success did not appear to transfer to his son John, who inherited Lindenwald and promptly ran it into the ground, forcing it to be sold. Our twelfth president had spent a lifetime restoring and caring for his beloved estate—only to have it lost soon after he died. If there is any consolation to his lapsed legacy, it may be the expression "OK," which apparently originated from his nickname, "Old Kinderhook," and which still lives on as one of the most popular phrases in the English language. Etymologists claim the earliest written references come from a Democratic Party slogan—"The OK Club"—which was used for Van Buren's re-election campaign of 1840. The phrase endures, but it was not sufficient to get him re-elected, however.

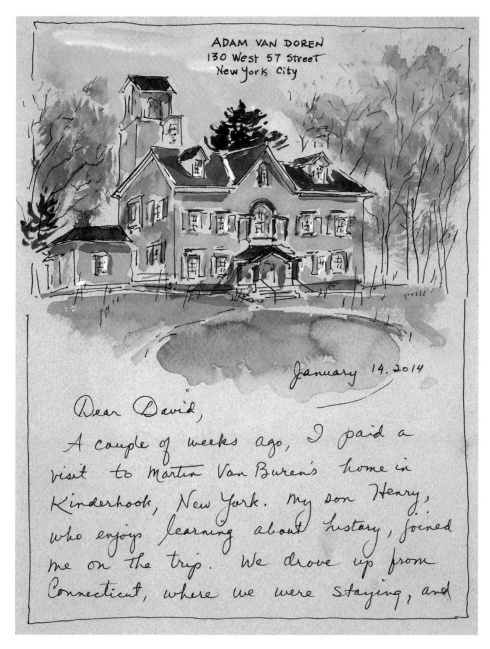

ADAM VAN DOREN
130 West 57 Street
New York City

January 14, 2014

Dear David,

A couple of weeks ago, I paid a visit to Martin Van Buren's home in Kinderhook, New York. My son Henry, who enjoys learning about history, joined me on the trip. We drove up from Connecticut, where we were staying, and

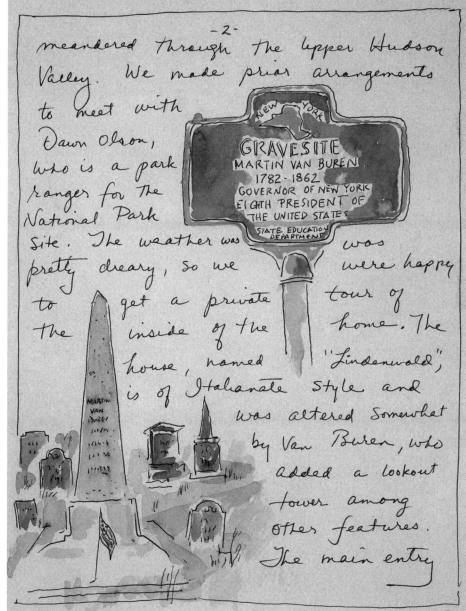

GRAVESITE
MARTIN VAN BUREN
1782-1862
GOVERNOR OF NEW YORK
EIGHTH PRESIDENT OF
THE UNITED STATES
STATE EDUCATION
DEPARTMENT

meandered through the Upper Hudson Valley. We made prior arrangements to meet with Dawn Olson, who is a park ranger for The National Park Site. The weather was pretty dreary, so we was were happy to get a private tour of the inside of the home. The house, named "Lindenwald", is of Italianate style and was altered somewhat by Van Buren, who added a lookout tower among other features. The main entry hall is adorned with an elaborate mural, of a pastoral scene, and it surrounds the entire room above the wainscotting. Van Buren opened up some of the walls in the room to make it large enough to fit a long table for festive dinner parties. A wide "Dutch door," with wrought iron hinges, marks the entrance. The parlor and other living quarters do not have very much original

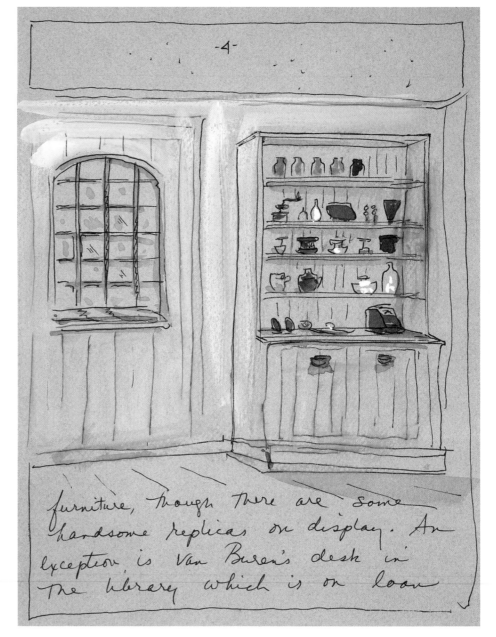

furniture, though there are some handsome replicas on display. An exception is Van Buren's desk in the library which is on loan

from The Smithsonian
Institution...
An
impressive
portrait of
the eighth
president
is on
display above
one of the
marble
fireplaces.

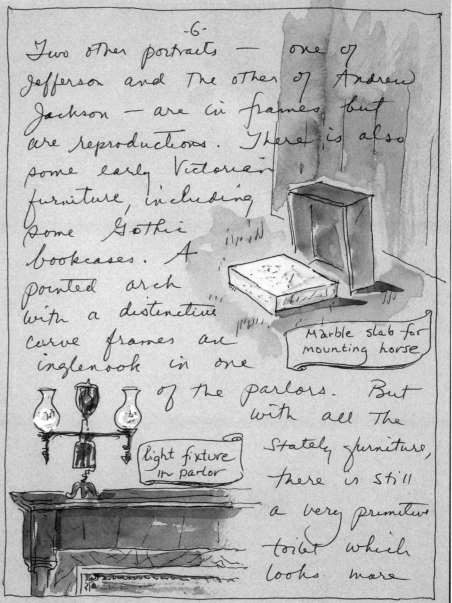

6

Two other portraits — one of
Jefferson and the other of Andrew
Jackson — are in frames, but
are reproductions. There is also
some early Victorian
furniture, including
some Gothic
bookcases. A
pointed arch
with a distinctive
curve frames an
inglenook in one
of the parlors. But
with all the
stately furniture,
there is still
a very primitive
toilet which
looks more

Marble slab for
mounting horse

light fixture
in parlor

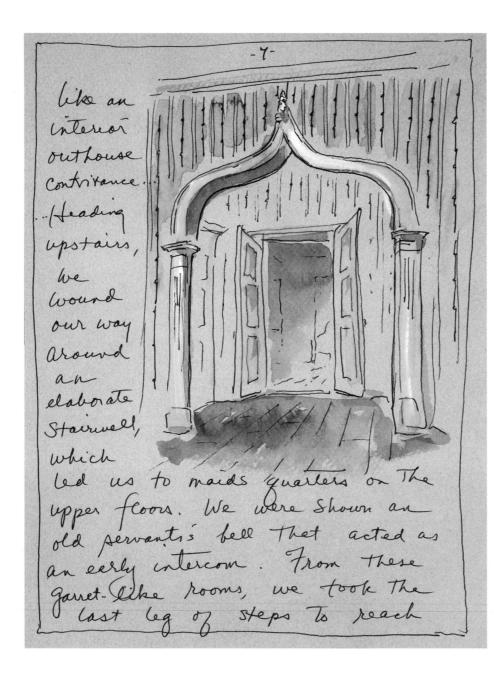

like an interior outhouse contrivance... Heading upstairs, we wound our way around an elaborate stairwell, which led us to maids quarters on the upper floors. We were shown an old servant's bell that acted as an early intercom. From these garret-like rooms, we took the last leg of steps to reach

the tower which affords handsome views of the surrounding landscape. Though it is clear that much of Van Buren's original estate has

"toilet"

servants' bell

lost some of its luster, there still are some substantial hay fields which are still part of the historic site... After Van Buren

died, his son inherited the property but apparently went bankrupt within a year and was forced to sell it. The residence was later purchased by the Park Service. They are involved in several restoration projects at the moment... Van Buren was known for being short and we were able to see the marble block outside which he used to mount his horse. Known as

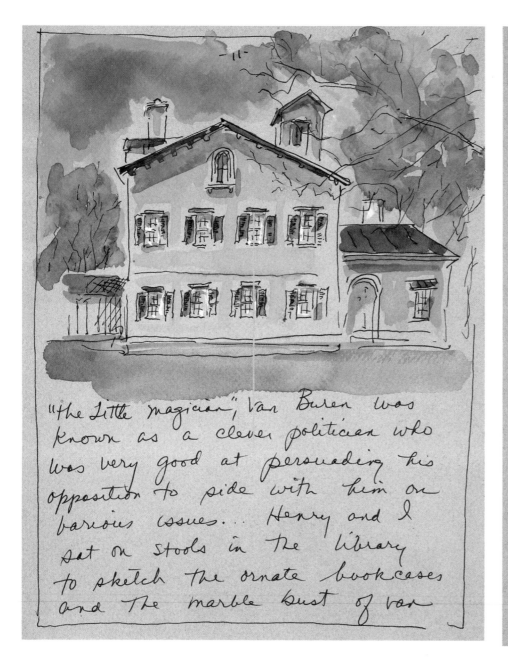

-11-

"the little magician", Van Buren was known as a clever politician who was very good at persuading his opposition to side with him on various issues... Henry and I sat on stools in the library to sketch the ornate bookcases and the marble bust of van

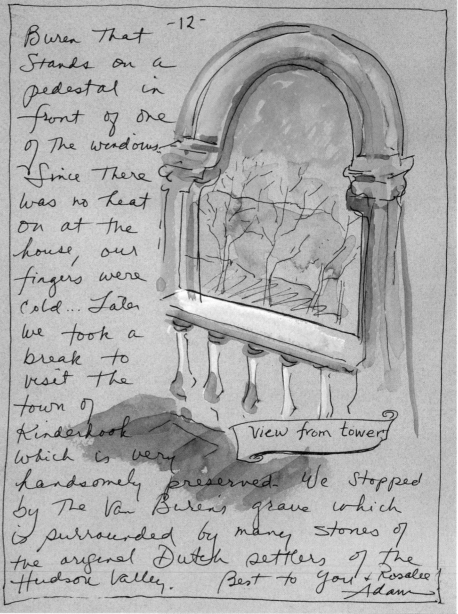

-12-

Buren that stands on a pedestal in front of one of the windows. Since there was no heat on at the house, our fingers were cold... Later we took a break to visit the town of Kinderhook which is very handsomely preserved. We stopped by the Van Buren's grave which is surrounded by many stones of the original Dutch settlers of the Hudson Valley. Best to you & Rosalee, Adam

View from tower

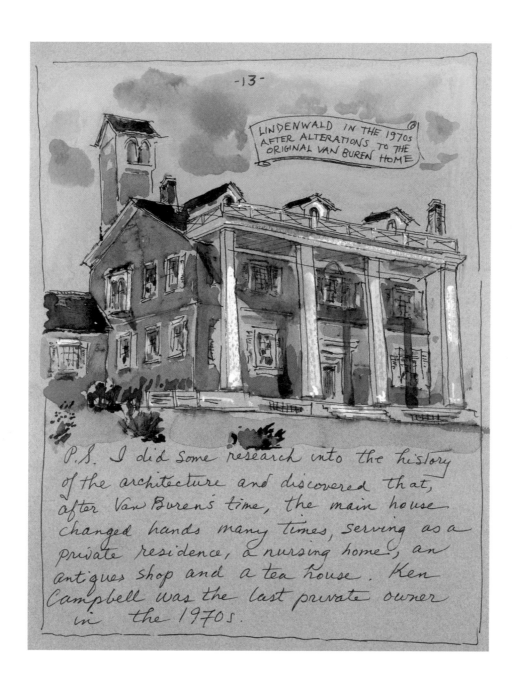

-13-

LINDENWALD IN THE 1970s AFTER ALTERATIONS TO THE ORIGINAL VAN BUREN HOME

P.S. I did some research into the history of the architecture and discovered that, after Van Buren's time, the main house changed hands many times, serving as a private residence, a nursing home, an antiques shop and a tea house. Ken Campbell was the last private owner in the 1970s.

HARRY TRUMAN HOME, INDEPENDENCE, MISSOURI

HARRY S. TRUMAN (1884-1972)

[term of office: 1945-1953]

"AMAZING GRACE" was serenading me from a nearby church tower the day I arrived at the Higher Ground, a small hotel conveniently located across the street from the Harry S. Truman historic site. The Christian hymn made me think of Truman himself, who was also "lost" once, without prospects, but overcame great odds to become a hero. The white gingerbread Victorian, where Harry and his wife Bess first courted, sits on a small lot, surrounded by other houses with similarly small lots. I was struck by how little privacy there was and wondered if it bothered the Trumans. "They were used to neighbors, having grown up in Independence," one of the park rangers, Jeff Wade, told me, "But it got pretty difficult when he returned from the presidency. Thrill seekers stole pieces of the lawn, and even parts of his house." Truman was forced to install a wrought iron gate (which the government paid for) to protect his property, a reluctant concession to celebrity culture.

I staked a corner of Delaware Street, where I could sketch the ornate front porch, the mansard roof, and the elaborate cornice. I imagined dinner guests in the 1920s arriving with hot apple pie, big hats, and long dresses. Independence was a lot smaller then, but even when it expanded, Truman still loved it. "It's just as good a place as there is, and they don't make them any better," he said.

In his retirement, the former president relished his daily walks around town and started the Early Risers' Walking Society. Fortunately, I didn't have a car, so I was able to experience myself what those walks were like. Heading toward Main Street, the small, well-kept bungalows gradually gave way to slightly larger office buildings, and then to the courthouse where Truman worked as a judge. A statue of Andrew Jackson on the courthouse lawn was a reminder that Missouri was still very much a southern state.

The soda shop (now called "Clinton's") where Truman once worked still stands on the corner, and I went in to get a refreshing egg cream. "I tried never to forget who I was and where I'd come from," Truman once said, and those rock-solid, midwestern values must have been a source of strength when he faced difficult world challenges as president. Hiroshima, the Korean War, McCarthyism, steel and coal strikes, the Berlin airlift—all would require wrenching decisions for which he accepted full responsibility. "The buck stops here" will always be remembered as his slogan.

The best evidence of what Truman was truly like can be found inside his house. The Park Service has painstakingly preserved every item exactly as it was left when Bess died (she outlived Harry by ten years), down to the cracked linoleum on the kitchen floor, and the chipped paint by the back door. (The Trumans were not wealthy people; there were no presidential retirement benefits then and so they lived on his World War I army pension instead). Even the daily calendar above the toaster is frozen in time in 1982. I could almost smell the fresh roasted coffee—about which Bess was very particular—cornmeal dumplings, and turnip greens, favorites from their Missouri upbringing. The president also had a weakness for sorghum molasses, a local treat, but he was basically a self-described "meat and potatoes man." He learned in the army to eat what was put in front of him. "In my outfit, when a man kicked about his food, he was given a chance to improve it. That soon cured the kickers!"

In the library, Bess and Harry's reading chairs still have their favorite books on the side tables; hers was the Dorothy Sayers mystery *Strong Poison*, and his *A Stillness at Appomattox* by Bruce Catton. "A leader must also be a reader," he once wrote, and it was revealing to peruse the books on his shelves. There was the complete Shakespeare and all of Mark Twain. Other interesting titles I noted included everything from Jacques Barzun's *Teacher in America* and John Kenneth Galbraith's *The Great Crash* to Carl Sandburg's *Abraham Lincoln* and Mao Tse-Tung's *Quotations*.

You can still see the stains on the wallpaper where Harry routinely held onto the wall when lifting himself out of his low-cushioned chair. Harry's coat and Fedora continue to hang on a hook by the side door. In the main hall, a full length portrait of his daughter Margaret, Harry's pride and joy, presides near the front entrance. It reminded me of how close the Truman family was. One Park Service guide, Matt Turner told me Margaret visited in the 1990s, not having been back for many years, and that she was quite moved and "emotional" after such a long absence. In the front parlor is the family piano, which Truman loved to play, with his Chopin waltzes still on the music stand. His spirit was so alive in the house, so watchful; I hoped that if I waited long enough, he might just stroll in the door and begin tinkling the ivories for old times' sake. People like Harry live on vividly in memory.

My last stop was the garage at the back of the house. It still had Truman's 1972 Chrysler Newport with 19,000 miles on it. Unfortunately the car had a cloth cover protecting it, and I couldn't convince the ranger to pull it off. But I could just make out the license plate which read 5745—May 7, 1945—the date of Germany's surrender in World War II.

Give 'em hell Harry!

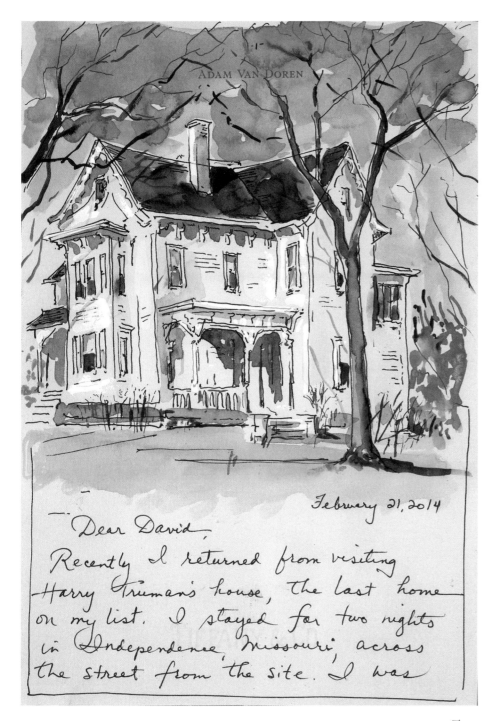

February 21, 2014

Dear David,

Recently I returned from visiting
Harry Truman's house, the last home
on my list. I stayed for two nights
in Independence, Missouri, across
the street from the site. I was

surprised to see how close the
house on Delaware Street is to its
neighbors. It was a pleasure to see
so many original contents in the
home, and to see how well
preserved they are. Even a patch
of wallpaper was kept untouched
in the kitchen where Harry

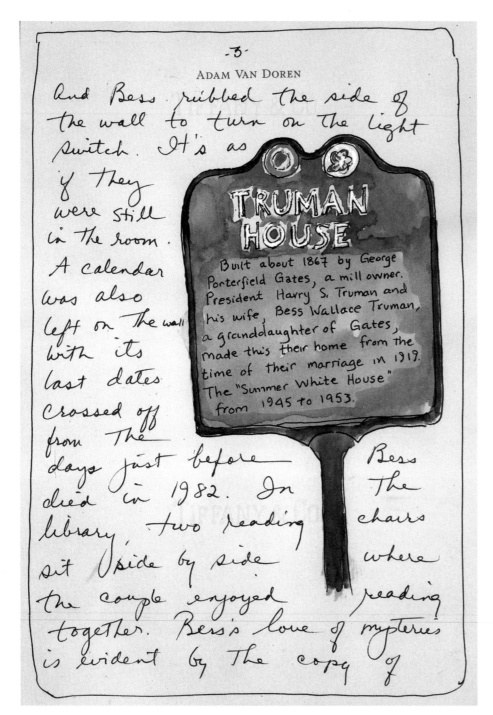

and Bess rubbed the side of the wall to turn on the light switch. It's as if they were still in the room. A calendar was also left on the wall with its last dates crossed off from the days just before died in 1982. In the library, two reading sit side by side. the couple enjoyed together. Bess's love of mysteries is evident by the copy of

Bess the chairs where reading

TRUMAN HOUSE

Built about 1867 by George Porterfield Gates, a mill owner. President Harry S. Truman and his wife, Bess Wallace Truman, a granddaughter of Gates, made this their home from the time of their marriage in 1919. The "Summer White House" from 1945 to 1953.

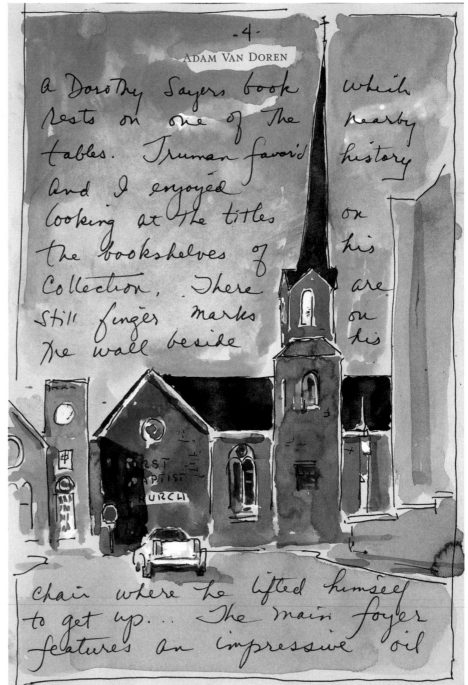

a Dorothy Sayers book rests on one of the tables. Truman favored and I enjoyed looking at the titles the bookshelves of collection. There still finger marks the wall beside

which nearby history on his are on his

chair where he lifted himself to get up... The main foyer features an impressive oil

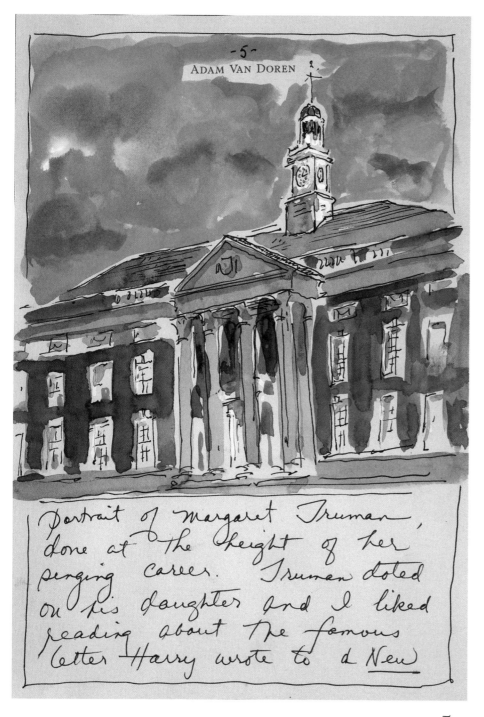

5

ADAM VAN DOREN

portrait of margaret Truman,
done at the height of her
singing career. Truman doted
on his daughter and I liked
reading about the famous
letter Harry wrote to a <u>New</u>

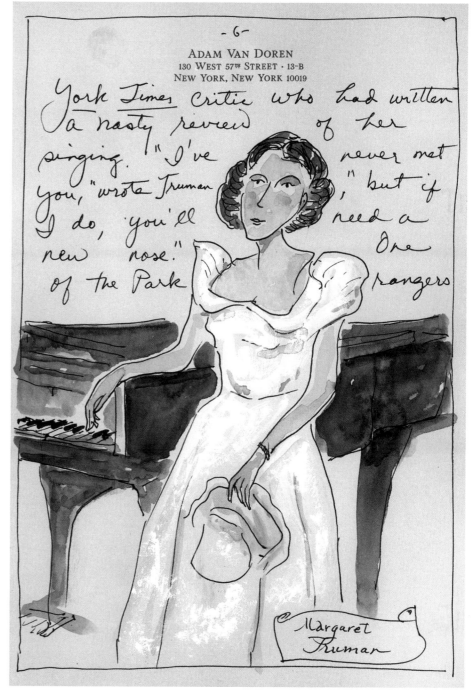

ADAM VAN DOREN
130 WEST 57TH STREET · 13-B
NEW YORK, NEW YORK 10019

York <u>Times</u> critic who had written
a nasty review of her
singing. "I've never met
you," wrote Truman ," but if
I do, 'you'll need a
new nose." One
of the Park rangers

Margaret
Truman

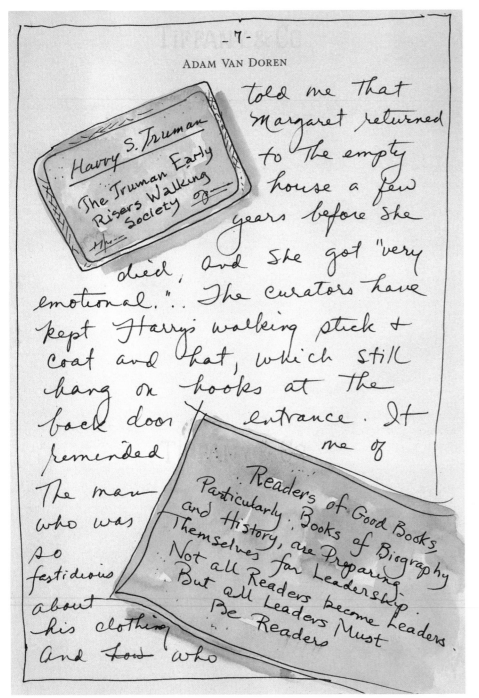

told me that Margaret returned to the empty house a few years before she died, and she got "very emotional."... The curators have kept Harry's walking stick + coat and hat, which still hang on hooks at the back door entrance. It reminded me of

The man who was so festidious about his clothing and ~~how~~ who

opened up a clothing store as one of his early ventures... The piano in the living room was a pleasure to see, considering how much Harry loved music. The ranger Matt Turner told me it was originally bought for Margaret

After Thomas Hart
Benton's Mural in the
Truman Library

but she
was disappointed
not to receive
a train set instead... The
back porch is enclosed and
looks out onto a main road,
without much privacy This
time of year. Bushes were
planted so that there was
more of a buffer during

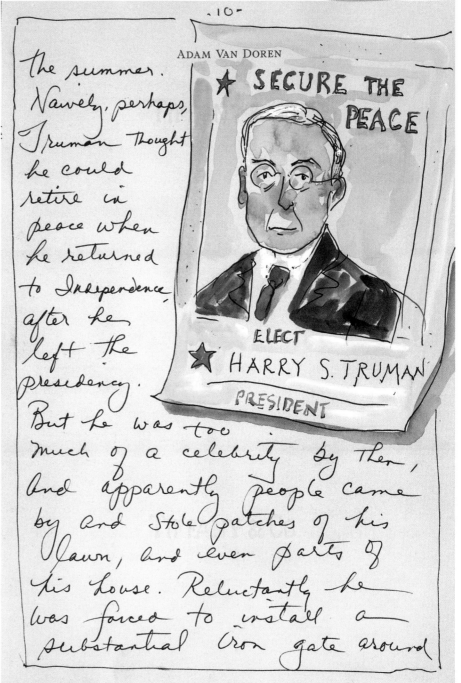

the summer.
Naively, perhaps,
Truman thought
he could
retire in
peace when
he returned
to Independence,
after he
left the
presidency.
But he was too
much of a celebrity by then,
and apparently people came
by and stole patches of his
lawn, and even parts of
his house. Reluctantly he
was forced to install a
substantial iron gate around

11

ADAM VAN DOREN

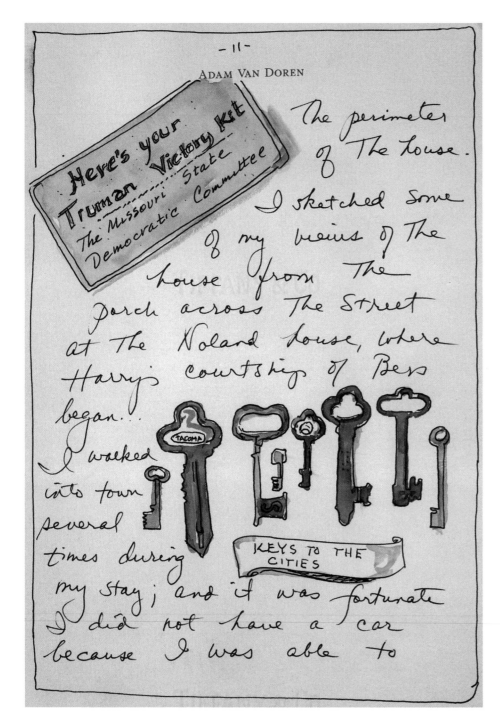

The perimeter of The house.

I sketched some of my views of The house from The porch across The street at The Noland house, where Harry's courtship of Bess began...

I walked into town several times during my stay; and it was fortunate I did not have a car because I was able to

KEYS TO THE CITIES

12

ADAM VAN DOREN

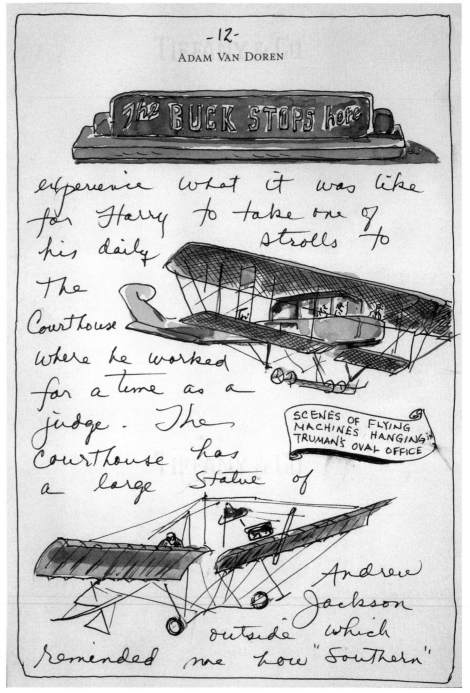

The BUCK STOPS here

experience what it was like for Harry to take one of his daily strolls to the Courthouse where he worked for a time as a judge. The Courthouse has a large statue of

SCENES OF FLYING MACHINES HANGING in TRUMAN'S OVAL OFFICE

Andrew Jackson outside which reminded me how "Southern"

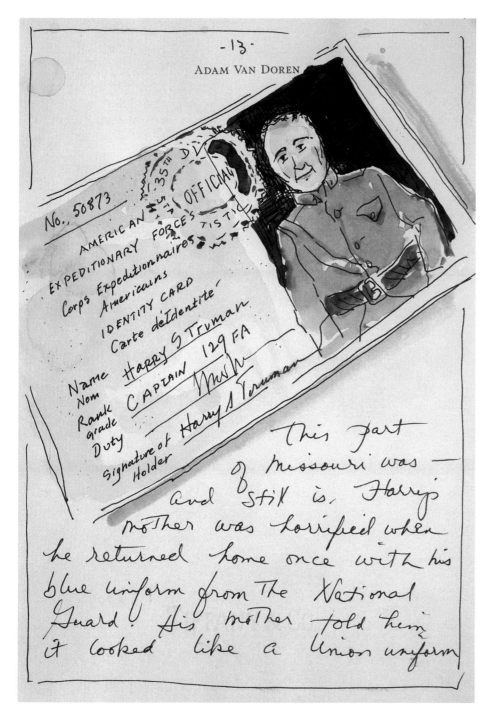

No. 50873

AMERICAN
EXPEDITIONARY FORCES
Corps Expeditionnaires
Americains
IDENTITY CARD
Carte de Identité

Name
Nom HARRY S TRUMAN

Rank
grade CAPTAIN 129 FA

Duty

Signature of Harry S Truman
Holder

This part
of Missouri was —
and still is. Harry's
mother was horrified when
he returned home once with his
blue uniform from The National
Guard! His mother told him
it looked like a Union uniform

Whistle Stop Campaign   during the
Crestline, Ohio 1948   Civil War, and
                                          she told him
never to wear it in her
house again... I met one

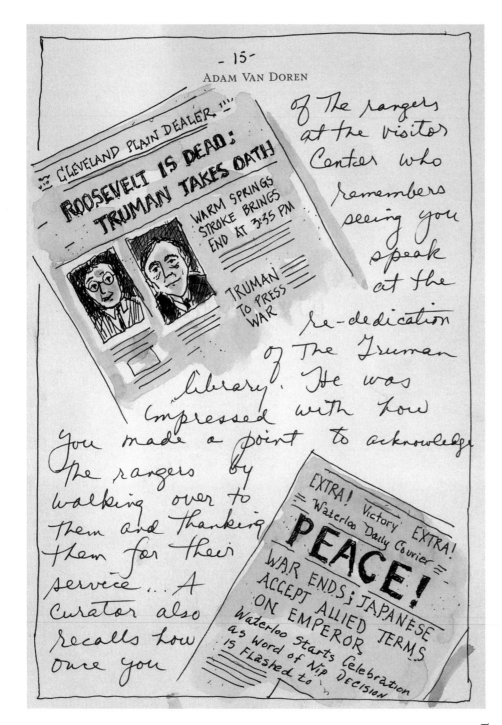

of the rangers at the visitors Center who remembers seeing you speak at the re-dedication of The Truman "library". He was impressed with how you made a point to acknowledge the rangers by walking over to them and thanking them for their service ... A curator also recalls how once you

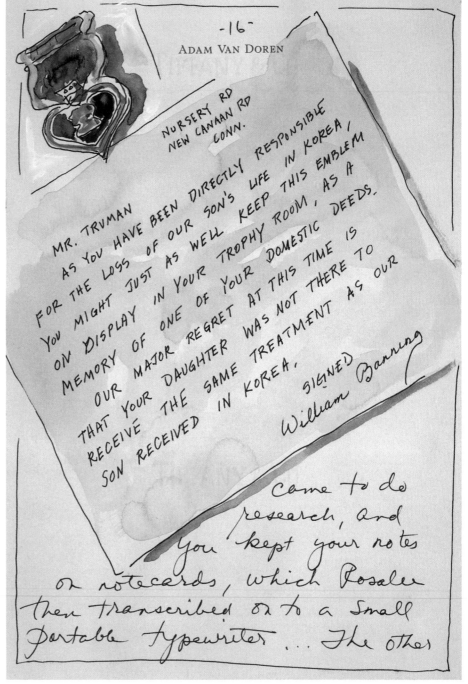

NURSERY RD
NEW CANAAN RD
CONN.

MR. TRUMAN
AS YOU HAVE BEEN DIRECTLY RESPONSIBLE FOR THE LOSS OF OUR SON'S LIFE IN KOREA, YOU MIGHT JUST AS WELL KEEP THIS EMBLEM ON DISPLAY IN YOUR TROPHY ROOM, AS A MEMORY OF ONE OF YOUR DOMESTIC DEEDS. OUR MAJOR REGRET AT THIS TIME IS THAT YOUR DAUGHTER WAS NOT THERE TO RECEIVE THE SAME TREATMENT AS OUR SON RECEIVED IN KOREA.

SIGNED
William Banning

came to do research, and you kept your notes on notecards, which Rosalee then transcribed on to a small portable typewriter ... The other

ADAM VAN DOREN

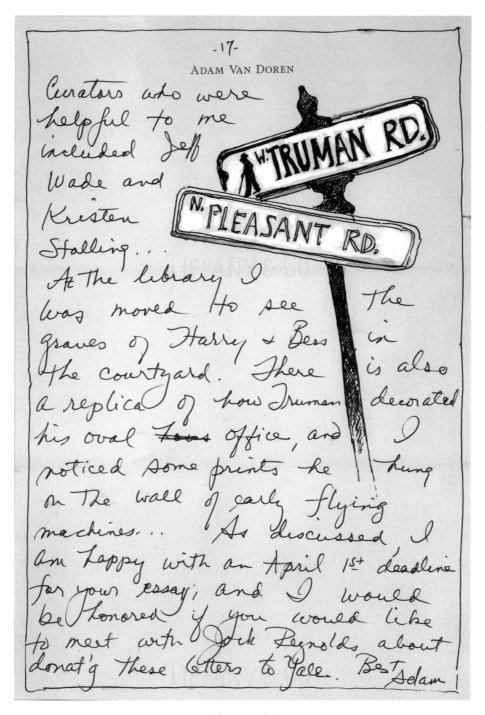

Curators who were helpful to me included Jeff Wade and Kristen Stalling...

At the library I was moved to see the graves of Harry & Bess in the courtyard. There is also a replica of how Truman decorated his oval ~~foss~~ office, and I noticed some prints he hung on the wall of early flying machines...

As discussed, I am happy with an April 1st deadline for your essay; and I would be honored if you would like to meet with Jock Reynolds about donat'g these letters to Yale. Best

Adam

PRAIRIE CHAPEL RANCH, CRAWFORD, TEXAS

GEORGE W. BUSH (1946-)

[*term of office: 2001-2009*]

IF THERE IS STILL such a place as a one-horse town in this day and age, then Crawford must be it. Located in the western part of Texas, this small corner of McLennan County is little more than a gas station, a sandwich shop and a few sleepy stores. It was my first trip to the Longhorn state, and I arrived there in late April by way of Fort Worth and Waco. My final destination was Prairie Chapel Ranch, but the GPS in my rental car could not locate it. Fortunately, I had a good map and followed the serpentine roads till I reached a stone barrier with bright red letters that read STOP. A member of the Secret Service was prepared for my arrival and gave me a Texas welcome with a big smile and a strong handshake.

I was asked to follow a jeep up to the main house, which is secluded and set a good ways back in the two-thousand-acre spread. Laura Bush greeted me in the driveway and graciously invited me in. The modern house is a long rectangle, set low to the ground with beige stone, high ceilings, French doors, and plenty of light. Clean lines, built-in bookcases, and contemporary furniture give a fresh look to the rooms. Outdoors, Laura was pleased to show me the just-bloomed bluebonnets, and was quick to point out that

the bluebonnet is the state flower of Texas. She gave me the lay of the land and told me I could paint wherever I wanted.

This was easier said than done. The ecofriendly structure blends so naturally and modestly into the landscape that I could hardly tell it was there. This discreet, almost self-effacing sleekness was not exactly what I expected from a family of such wealth and prominence. Stretching around me on all sides, the ranch's vast landscape unfurled with open fields, a lake, gnarled old trees, cacti, and many semi-arid plants I had never seen before. In the distance, I could make out a thick limestone cross, set upon a heavy carved stone like an open-air altar. (I learned later it weighs over a ton, and was designed specifically for the wedding of the Bushes' daughter Jenna to Henry Hager in 2008).

About an hour after I staked my location and began working with my paint and brushes, I noticed someone wearing casual work clothes coming toward me. Was it a gardener? Another member of the Secret Service? No, it was George W. himself. His casual demeanor quickly put me at ease, and we shook hands. We talked about my book project, the other presidents' homes I'd painted, our mutual connections to Yale, and finally about his own painting, which he has taken up seriously. He invited me back inside the house to see his canvases, which were lined up along his living room and bedroom walls.

They comprise a substantial body of work. He told me he had plans to build a studio for himself, but he had not yet finalized the designs. There were portraits of animals, family members, politicians, and even some Ethiopian tribesmen from his recent trip to Africa. We spoke of painters we admired. The forty-third president told me he liked Fairfield Porter and Alex Katz. We then discussed the age-old challenges of composition and color. There was nothing pretentious about our chat. When I asked him if he had read any of the reviews of his work, such as the cover story in the *New York Times* about a recent exhibit, he emphasized that he doesn't pay much attention to these articles. He said he had been reviewed most of his life in one form or another and that he was just interested in becoming the best painter he could be.

It was an exalting experience, to say the least, to be on a first-name basis with the former president, and engaged in such a relaxed, informal conversation with a person who has shaped the nation's history. But George W. seems fully removed from public life, and has been enjoying reading the book *Painting as a Pastime*, by another public figure who took up painting in retirement, Winston Churchill. "W" told one reporter in a newspaper recently that he was not especially interested in talking about politics these days but was more than happy to talk about art. Bush now joins Eisenhower and Jimmy Carter, who both took up painting after life at the White House.

When it was time to part ways, he and I shook hands, and I headed back outdoors. The former president apologized for not being able to spend more time with me, but he had to go to Dallas—his primary residence—for another appointment. He said he had enjoyed our visit and offered that perhaps I might return to give him a watercolor lesson. (In time, I would return to do exactly that, but that exchange is "off the record." I will simply report that he was a very good student).

Leaving the Bushes to pack up for their departure, I resumed my painting from the lawn, with what was left of the day's sunlight. By late afternoon I had completed my work and it was time to return to New York. As I headed for my rental car, one of the Secret Service officers, who also doubles as a caretaker for the property, kindly invited me to join him in his jeep and take a quick tour of the ranch. We rumbled along a rugged trail—used mostly by "W" on his mountain bike—and bounced up and down as we passed through acres of tall grass and milkweed, which Mrs. Bush cultivates to attract Monarch butterflies. We maneuvered several switchbacks before careening down to a shallow creek by the edge of a steep embankment. A hidden grotto, deep in the woods, came into view, with a picturesque waterfall cascading over prehistoric rocks. The agent informed me that Bush sometimes took foreign leaders to meet with him at this tranquil spot. I marveled at the beauty of the scenery, and the unforgettable colors of the stone. Too bad it was time to go; I got the sudden urge to pull out my brushes and paint some more.

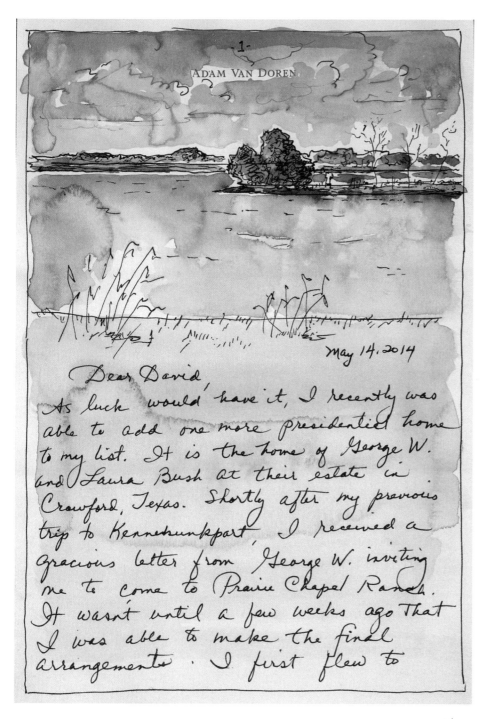

ADAM VAN DOREN

May 14, 2014

Dear David,

As luck would have it, I recently was able to add one more presidential home to my list. It is the home of George W. and Laura Bush at their estate in Crawford, Texas. Shortly after my previous trip to Kennebunkport, I received a gracious letter from George W. inviting me to come to Prairie Chapel Ranch. It wasn't until a few weeks ago that I was able to make the final arrangements. I first flew to

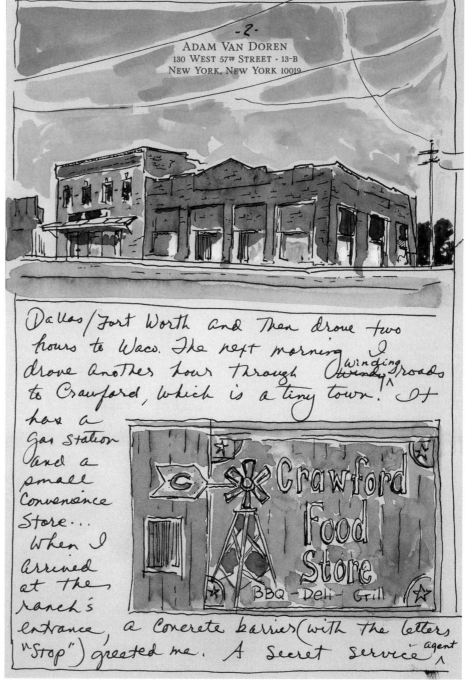

ADAM VAN DOREN
130 WEST 57TH STREET · 13-B
NEW YORK, NEW YORK 10019

Dallas/Fort Worth and then drove two hours to Waco. The next morning I drove another hour through winding roads to Crawford, which is a tiny town. It has a gas station and a small convenience store... When I arrived at the ranch's entrance, a concrete barrier (with the letters "Stop") greeted me. A Secret service agent

Crawford Food Store
BBQ - Deli - Grill

[143]

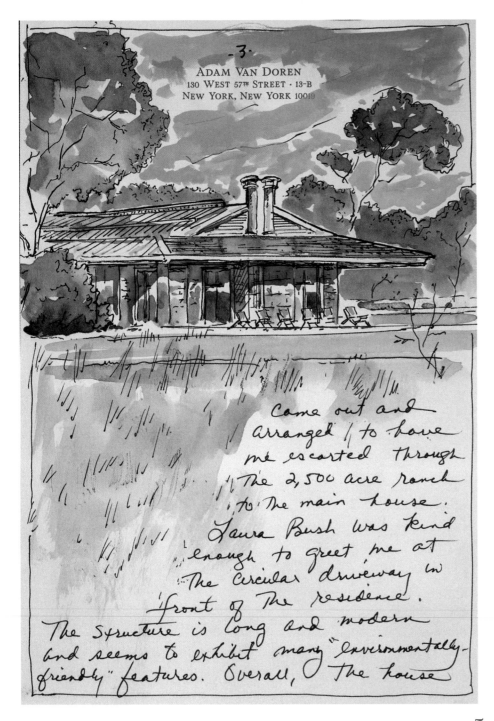

ADAM VAN DOREN
130 WEST 57TH STREET · 13-B
NEW YORK, NEW YORK 10019

Came out and arranged to have me escorted through the 2,500 acre ranch to the main house. Laura Bush was kind enough to greet me at the circular driveway in front of the residence.

The structure is long and modern and seems to exhibit many "environmentally-friendly" features. Overall, the house

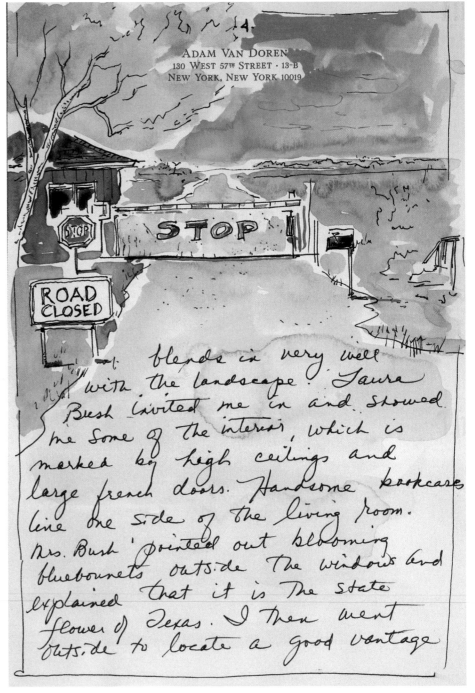

ADAM VAN DOREN
130 WEST 57TH STREET · 13-B
NEW YORK, NEW YORK 10019

blends in very well with the landscape. Laura Bush invited me in and showed me some of the interior, which is marked by high ceilings and large french doors. Handsome bookcases line one side of the living room. Mrs. Bush pointed out blooming bluebonnets outside the windows and explained that it is the state flower of Texas. I then went outside to locate a good vantage

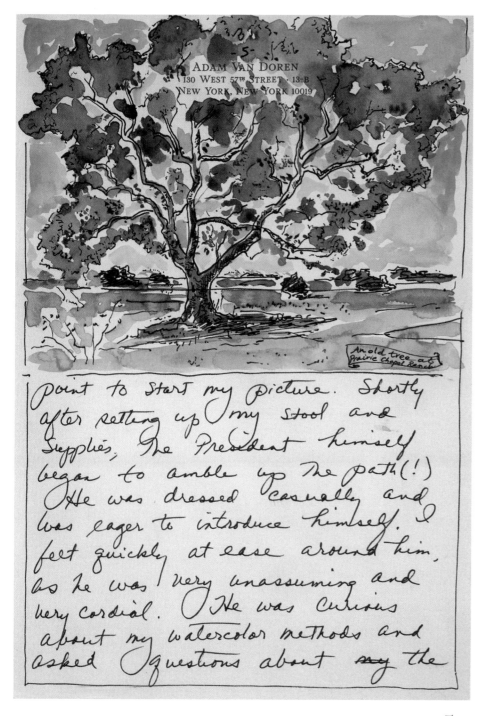

ADAM VAN DOREN
130 WEST 57TH STREET · 13-B
NEW YORK, NEW YORK 10019

An old tree at
Prairie Chapel Ranch

point to start my picture. Shortly
after setting up my stool and
supplies, the President himself
began to amble up the path(!)
He was dressed casually and
was eager to introduce himself. I
felt quickly at ease around him,
as he was very unassuming and
very cordial. He was curious
about my watercolor methods and
asked ~~my~~ questions about the

ADAM VAN DOREN

other presidential homes I had
painted. We also discussed that
I was teaching art at Yale, where
he had gone to college. The
President seemed very easy-going
and we naturally segwayed into the
topic of his own painting, which
he takes very seriously, and which
has been a principal occupation
in his "retirement." He invited
me back into his house to see

some of his work. Several canvases
leaned up against the wall
in his bedroom. They were
unframed and recently completed.
One was from a recent trip he
had taken to Ethiopia. He
then showed me more of his
work on his Ipad. There were
several impressive portraits of
animals. I singled out one that
I thought was particularly well

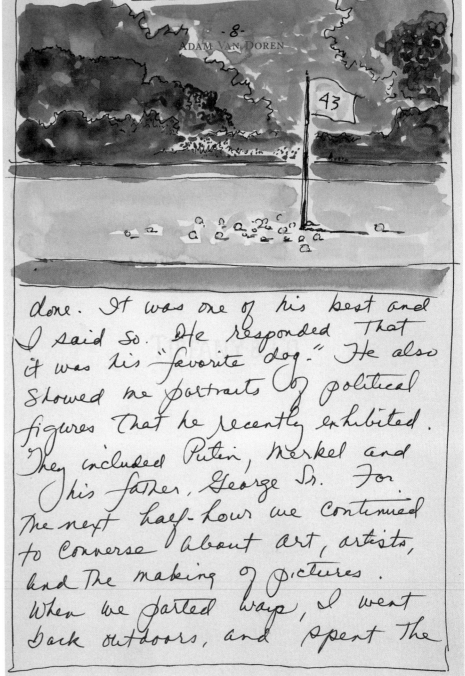

done. It was one of his best and
I said so. He responded that
it was his "favorite dog." He also
showed me portraits of political
figures that he recently exhibited.
They included Putin, Merkel and
his father, George Sr. For
the next half-hour we continued
to converse about art, artists,
and the making of pictures.
When we parted ways, I went
back outdoors, and spent the

ADAM VAN DOREN

rest of the afternoon working on my picture. George and Laura soon thereafter left for Dallas where they have their primary residence... The sun which had been hiding all morning, suddenly came out with a vengeance and I sought the shade of an old tree near the house. A small one-hole golf-course was nearby with a flag at the hole which read the number "43." By late afternoon, it started to rain and agent Robert Blossom escorted me out. We saw lovely grottoes + creeks on the way back...

Best to you + Rosalee, Adam

JIMMY CARTER HISTORIC SITE, PLAINS, GEORGIA

JIMMY CARTER (1924-)

[term of office: 1977-1981]

Peanuts. Fried peanuts. Boiled peanuts. Cajun peanuts. Peanut ice cream. I tried them all on my recent visit to Plains, Georgia, to meet with former president Jimmy Carter and to see his birthplace. I arrived at the tiny town (pop. 675) by flying first into Atlanta, then driving southwest three hours along the Ocmulgee River, past acres of cotton fields, peach orchards, and rows and rows of sugar cane. I traveled through places with names like Oglethorpe, Montezuma, and Americus.

Plains, originally Plains of Dura (after a city in the Bible), has been home to Carter for all his ninety years, except mostly for his sojourns at the naval academy and the White House. He was raised a mile from downtown on a peanut farm—what else?—and his boyhood home is a national historic site, as are his former high school, the Baptist church where he still teaches Sunday school, the nursing center where his mother Lillian worked, and the gas station his brother Billy owned (remember Billy Beer?). I felt like I had entered a Jimmy Carter version of Garrison Keillor's Lake Wobegon. Indeed local shopkeepers have made a cottage industry of selling Carter souvenirs, from campaign buttons to coffee mugs and even a bobblehead doll.

This was my first trip to the Deep South, and the ninety-two degree heat—a near record for October—was a humid reminder. I spent most of my days at Carter's birthplace, painting and sketching his family's old house on seventeen acres of what was once a 360-acre farm. The modest Sears Roebuck bungalow—sold by Carter's parents Earl and Lillian in 1941 before being purchased by the National Parks in 1992—has a central "shotgun" hallway, designed to catch the breezes, and is flanked by a series of small spaces that include bedrooms for Jimmy and his siblings Gloria, Ruth, and Billy. The bathroom is primitive, with just a bucket on a string for cold water, but it was considered a luxury in the 1930s when the Carters first got running water. The furniture in the home is not original, but Carter actually constructed one of the replicas himself, a wooden table called "mother" because Lillian would often leave notes on it for the family. Unfortunately there are no original artifacts in the house as they were removed in 1941 when the house was sold.

Outdoors, the small dwelling is surrounded by a large grove of pecan trees, a windmill, a blacksmith shop, a chicken shed, and a mule barn. There is even a clay tennis court, which ranger Kevin Alexander explained to me: "All you had to do was scrape the ground: this part of Georgia is all red clay." Carter is even more poignant about this characteristic of his home in his memoir *An Hour Before Daylight* : "My most persistent impression as a farm boy was of the earth. There was a closeness, almost an immersion in the sand, and loam, and red clay that seemed natural and constant. The soil caressed my bare feet, and the dust was always boiling up from the dirt road that passed fifty feet from our front door."

On my last day in Plains, the big moment had arrived. I was scheduled to sit down with Carter in the late afternoon. Though I had met a living president before—George W. Bush—I was excited at the prospect of meeting another. Carter, elected in 1976, was the first president I remember well. His years are recalled for cardigan sweaters during the energy crisis, meetings at Camp David, a boycott of the Moscow Olympics, and, of course, the Iranian hostage crisis. But most of all I remember a decent, honest man of faith who was committed to peace and to diplomacy, even when it seemed hopeless. Carter seemed quite old to me back then, but it is sobering to think that when he served as president, he was exactly the same age I am now.

Arrangements for my interview with Jimmy, one of the first presidents to use his nickname formally, had been planned through Bob Graham, the former governor of Florida, whose granddaughter Caroline I had taught painting to at Yale. Graham in turn put me in touch with Jay Hakes, former director of the Jimmy Carter Presidential Library.

When I arrived at the Carter compound, located about two miles from where Jimmy was born, the Secret Service inspected my Hertz rental car before letting me proceed. Set in a shady woodland, the house is an unassuming yet pleasant ranch that the Carters built it in 1961 and have remained in ever since. An elderly woman on his staff answered the door and asked me to wait in the living room. After a few minutes President Carter walked in wearing a casual button-down shirt, and I suddenly felt overdressed in my jacket and tie. Carter, looking much younger than his age, sat down in a chair beside me. It was remarkable to be that close to a person who was once the most protected man in America. He apologized for not meeting me earlier, but he had been in Texas for Habitat for Humanity, and also campaigning upstate for his grandson Jason Carter who was running for governor of Georgia, a post Carter himself once held.

As we started talking about the past, his eyes lit up when he recounted his youth. I asked him about the railroad track across from his old house. "The freight trains would pass through twice a day. As kids we used to like to count all the cars, which often reached a hundred and forty."

"Did you see many hobos?" I asked.

"Yes, especially during the Depression when there was thirty percent unemployment. They would stop by our house and ask for work, for which they got a dollar a day, and they would mark on our mailbox with chalk to let other hobos know we were a safe bet."

We talked about, among other things, the difficulties of being a farmer these days ("It costs a hundred and sixty thousand dollars to buy a good tractor"); his favorite poet, Dylan Thomas; and his favorite president, Truman.

Carter then took me to the back of his house to show me his art studio where he has recently taken up oils, and he pulled down a limited edition book of another president—Eisenhower—who also painted in his spare time. When it was time to leave, Carter graciously signed his most recent book *A Call to Action: Women, Religion, Violence and Power*. "My twenty-eighth book," he said with pride. "It's how I make my living for the most part. I opted out of the lecture circuit after I left the White House." We then had a photo-op. A Secret Service officer snapped the picture as Carter and I shook hands. There was that famous grin again, the one that won him the election from a country that genuinely needed a smile after Watergate.

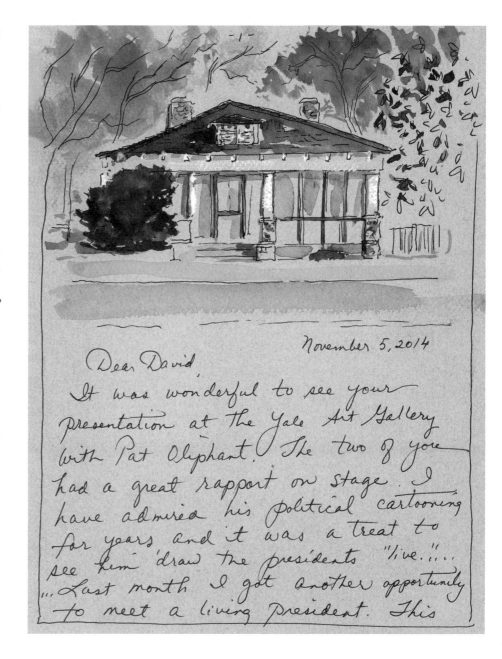

November 5, 2014

Dear David,

It was wonderful to see your presentation at the Yale Art Gallery with Pat Oliphant. The two of you had a great rapport on stage. I have admired his political cartooning for years and it was a treat to see him draw the presidents "live."...

...Last month I got another opportunity to meet a living president. This

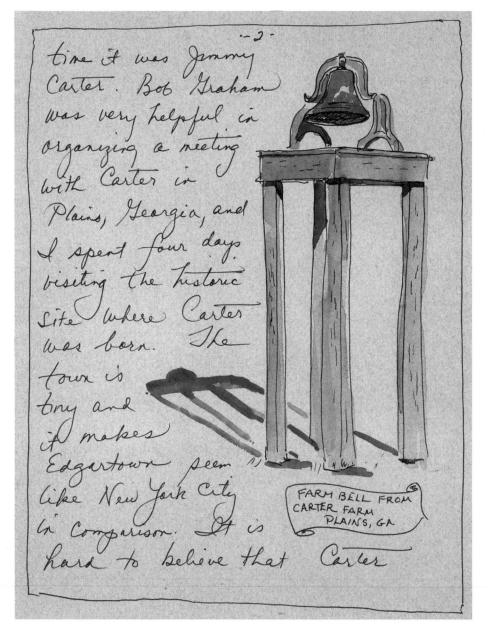

-2-

time it was Jimmy Carter. Bob Graham was very helpful in organizing a meeting with Carter in Plains, Georgia, and I spent four days visiting the historic site where Carter was born. The tour is tiny and it makes Edgartown seem like New York City in comparison. It is hard to believe that Carter

FARM BELL FROM
CARTER FARM
PLAINS, GA

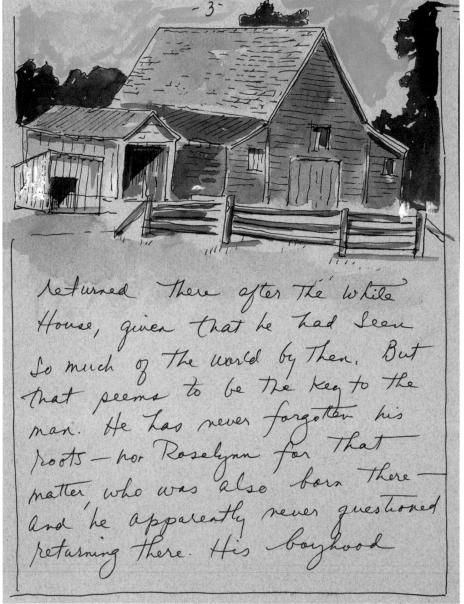

-3-

returned there after the White House, given that he had seen so much of the world by then. But that seems to be the key to the man. He has never forgotten his roots — nor Roselynn for that matter, who was also born there — and he apparently never questioned returning there. His boyhood

home is a modest
one, though not quite
as humble as some
earlier "log cabin"
presidents. There are
several, if not large,
rooms in the dwelling,
And the farm — at
least what remains
of it — has several
outbuildings, in-
cluding a privy
that the Carters used
before they got
running water. A few farm
animals, including goats and mules
are housed in one of the barns,

GAS PUMP

5

And I got a chance to
see them being
fed by one of
the Park rangers.
Next to the
house is a small
structure that Earl
(Carter's father) used as a store
to sell various goods, including
food he harvested on the farm.

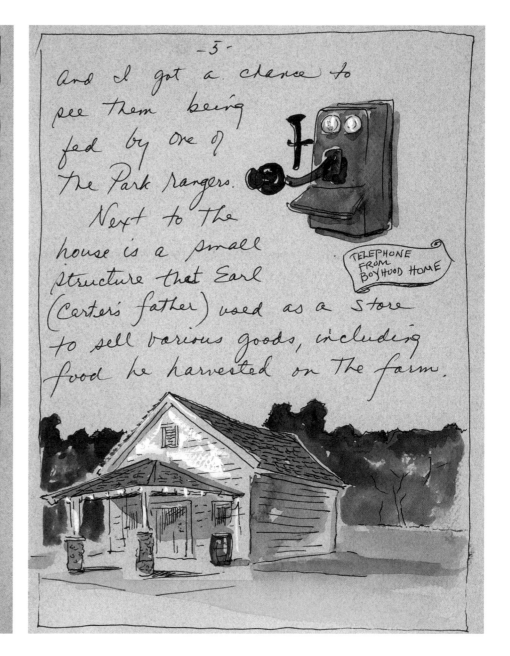

TELEPHONE
FROM
BOYHOOD HOME

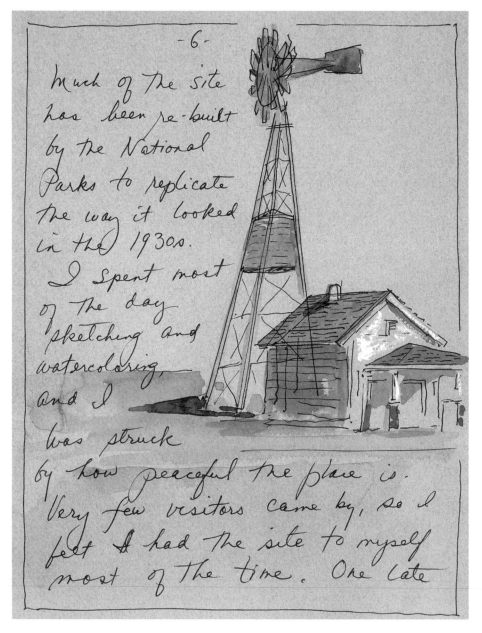

-6-

Much of the site has been re-built by the National Parks to replicate the way it looked in the 1930s.
I spent most of the day sketching and watercoloring, and I was struck by how peaceful the place is. Very few visitors came by, so I felt I had the site to myself most of the time. One late

-7-

afternoon, I sat by myself on the front porch of Carter's home, sharing the wood steps with a cat "Fraidy" who lives on the property... The railroad tracks across the road are a ghastly reminder of a time when trains were a vital part of American life. Carter no doubt heard the whistle in his bed at night.
On my last day I visited with Carter himself. I met him at the home he has

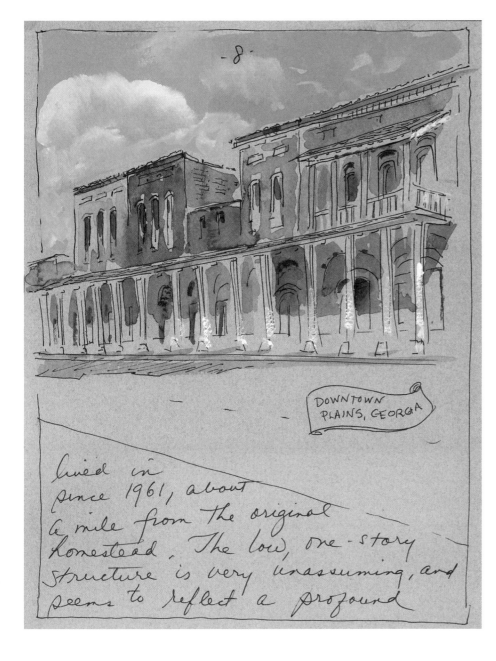

-8-

DOWNTOWN
PLAINS, GEORGIA

lived in
since 1961, about
a mile from the original
homestead. The low, one-story
structure is very unassuming, and
seems to reflect a profound

-9-

simplicity of Carter's character. I
was invited to sit with him
in his living room, and it was
exhilerating to see him in person
for the first time. He has a
gentle spirit, and was easy to
talk with. I enjoyed hearing
him talk of his past, and I
tried to keep our conversation
natural, without making it
into a formal "interview." I

could not help but think how this man was once at the center of so many world events, and yet still considered himself the "man from Plains."

When we parted, I thanked him, and returned to The Plains Inn where I spent my last night before heading back to NYC. I tried to think whether I could live in such a little hamlet, or whether it would be suffocating after a while. In the end I prefer the anonymity the city life offers, though it comes with a price(!) Best to you and Rosalee, Adam

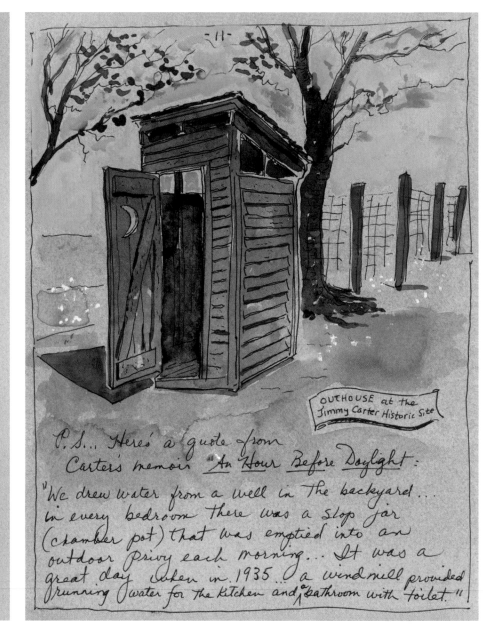

11

OUTHOUSE at the Jimmy Carter Historic Site

P.S... Here's a quote from Carter's memoir "An Hour Before Daylight:
"We drew water from a well in the backyard... in every bedroom there was a slop jar (chamber pot) that was emptied into an outdoor privy each morning... It was a great day when in 1935... a windmill provided running water for the kitchen and a bathroom with toilet."

EPILOGUE
THE WHITE HOUSE, WASHINGTON, DC

I CAN'T SAY I didn't try. For several months, I had been corresponding with John Stanwich, a National Park ranger, in hopes of gaining access to the White House. My goal was to paint a portrait of the rear façade, from the south lawn. My request was innocent enough, or so I thought. I hardly considered myself a security threat, plying my trade with a small set of watercolor paints, brushes, and paper. But I was naïve; we now live in an age of high anxiety.

"I wish I could help you," said a well-meaning Mr. Stanwich. "But the Secret Service will not allow you access to the grounds. The best I could suggest is that you paint from outside the gates."

"Do I need permission for that?" I asked, again the naïf.

"Yes, you will need to apply for a permit."

"But I am not organizing a rally or protesting."

"I realize that, but you will be in a stationary position for several hours and these are the regulations."

Gone are the days, I thought, when presidents like Andrew Jackson invited total strangers—without anything resembling an ID—

to "the people's house" for a reception in 1803. And sadly, there is just cause: recently an intruder scaled the White House gates and got as far as the East Room. Therefore I dutifully submitted my application and the next morning I met ranger Amy Dailey at the Zero Milestone marker (intended as the initial milestone from which all road distances in America should be calculated) at the north edge of President's Park. My heart sank when I saw how far I was from the White House—a football field away—but I was relieved to have secured the necessary clearances and to have been given the opportunity to paint. The sky was bright blue, and the sun made crisp, geometric shadows on my subject. The building, originally built in 1780 and modified in 1820 by Benjamin Latrobe, is a beautiful example of neo-Palladian classical architecture. Its Ionic columns, rusticated base, and triangular pediments are each articulated in a unified composition with restraint and grace. Looking at the landscaped gardens below the house, set among large mature trees, I thought of the first families' children who had played there, Caroline and John Kennedy, Jr., Amy Carter,

Chelsea Clinton, and now Sasha and Malia Obama. What a place to grow up! Their games outside must have been in stark contrast to the business their fathers faced inside.

Later that morning the weather turned and rain threatened, so I opted for a break and took a tour of the interior of the Executive Mansion, generously arranged by Stanwich. I joined a queue of tourists near a statue of General Sherman, and was scanned through three rounds of security checks. Once inside, I passed though a corridor with an exhibit of candid White House photos: there was LBJ in a chair with his head arched back, howling in the air with his dog; Nancy Reagan holding a shovel while planting a new mulberry tree; and four-year-old John Kennedy, Jr., in the Oval Office, popping his head out from under his father's desk.

A marble staircase led me to the main floor. The spacious rooms, each laid out in symmetrical succession, have ornate, coffered ceilings, columns, thick drapery, candle sconces, and exquisite antiques. Streams of sunlight flowed through the tall windows and spread across the parquet floors. I considered how every president, except Washington, had lived here—a remarkable fact given that the building burned in 1814 and then again in 1929. For some of these leaders, such as the Roosevelts, Kennedys, and Bushes, the grandeur of the White House may not have seemed imposing. They, after all, had each lived in quite substantial houses themselves. But for the Lincolns, Carters, Clintons, and Coolidges—"log cabin" presidents—the house was presumably a dramatic change. Was it intimidating? Did they feel worthy? I

wondered. For certain Chief Executives, the experience was less than glamorous. Taft called it the loneliest house in the world. Truman termed it a prison. And John Quincy Adams recalled his years there as the "four most miserable" of his life. I thought of Sebastian Flyte, the character in Evelyn Waugh's *Brideshead Revisited*, who despised his ancestral home because of its associations with a miserable childhood.

I imagine that it is nearly impossible to feel "at home" at 1600 Pennsylvania Avenue, given the intense scrutiny every president endures there. Between the ubiquitous video surveillance, Secret Service, and reporters—not to mention the job itself—there is rarely a moment of peace. Private residential quarters exist in the White House for the president's family, but I doubt *any* president experiences "privacy"—or many other normal trappings we enjoy in our personal lives for that matter. (As Truman put it, "If you want a friend in Washington, get a dog.")

I know that, for myself, I would feel inhibited making major decisions, or creating art, for that matter, with someone standing over my shoulder. It feels claustrophobic, stressful; and it restricts any spontaneous thinking. A president, though, has little choice. This may be the reason certain ones have spent so much time *away* from the White House. FDR liked to spend weeks at Warm Springs, Georgia, George W. Bush at the "Texas White House" in Crawford, Reagan at his Rancho del Cielo in California—and more recently, Obama in Hawaii.

On the other hand, there are presumably advantages to living like a sort of expatriate at the White House. Removed from the quiet confines of their own home, their "comfort zone", if you will, presidents must acquire a different, keener perspective of the world. Sometimes it is better to be on the outside looking in to fully appreciate and understand the critical issues America faces. Analogously, one of the most accurate accounts ever written about the United States, *Democracy in America*, was written by an outsider, Alexis de Tocqueville, who did not live here, but was a Frenchman visiting the United States in the 1800s. Yet so many of his takes on who we are still ring true today, including "I know of no country, indeed, where the love of money has taken stronger hold on the affections of men."

When I lived for several months in Venice, Italy, for instance, I saw Western civilization through a different lens. I began to consider how the Byzantine methods of choosing a Doge was not dissimilar, in principle, to our electoral college when electing the Chief Executive. I thought, too, of how Venetians live for art in ways that for the most part Americans often neither understand nor support. It is essential to the Italians' identity, their DNA, and it made me appreciate how culture can occasionally trump commerce.

As I continued my self-guided tour, I took note of the impressive art on the walls. There were the nineteenth-century Hudson River School painters, such as Thomas Moran, Albert Bierstadt, George Inness, and Jasper Cropsey. There were portraits of TR by John Singer Sargent, Benjamin Franklin by David Martin, Thomas Jefferson by Rembrandt Peale, Grace Coolidge by Howard Christy, and of course George Washington by Gilbert Stuart. I was pleased to see a painting of JFK by Aaron Shikler, a teacher of mine whom I first met in New York in a sketch group he co-founded fifty years ago. The portrait was painted in 1970, seven years after Kennedy died, but it is still a favorite among visitors. Kennedy is portrayed in a pensive pose with his head inclined downward. Shikler, now ninety-three, once told me that he wanted to capture the president's mood during a pivotal moment of his term, the Cuban Missile Crisis. "Since I couldn't paint him from life," the artist said, "I had to piece together carefully selected images from photographs, many which Teddy Kennedy provided."

In the Red Room, above one of the doors, I observed a dashing portrait from 1876 of Franklin Pierce by George P. A. Healy. The docent informed me that the nineteenth president's last remaining child, Benjamin, died shortly after the Pierces moved into the White House, and that his wife Jane was devastated. Pierce arranged for fresh-cut flowers to be delivered to the room every day to help console her. To this day, that tradition of daily bouquets continues.

In the East Room, a cavernous space with chandeliers and a grand piano, I saw the staff preparing for an upcoming reception. They would not disclose any details to me. I recognized the space from the TV press conferences that are often filmed there. Truman in his retirement was once invited by the Kennedys to a dinner in this room in 1961. The Man from Missouri, as he was often called, took one look at the lavish place settings, the mountains of food and wine, and lamented, "There goes democracy!"

In the State Dining Room, an inscription carved into the mantelpiece reads: MAY NONE BUT HONEST AND WISE MEN EVER RULE UNDER THIS ROOF. These words were taken from a letter John Adams wrote to his wife, Abigail, on November 2, 1800. Apparently FDR, shortly after taking up residence in the White House in 1933, discovered this missive hidden between the pages of a book he was reading in the library. Years later (and not surprisingly) Jackie Kennedy arranged for it to be inscribed above the fireplace.

On my way out of the White House, I asked one of the docents how the president conducted business in the rooms despite the intrusion of rope barriers and rolled-up carpets. "The tours only last till eleven thirty every day. After that everything is neatly put back in place so that official business can resume." Giving up any hope of catching a glimpse of Obama (he was vacationing in Martha's Vineyard), I exited past the portraits of George W. and Laura Bush, and headed back outdoors to finish my picture. Sitting on my folding stool, I swiveled around to see the view behind me of the Washington Monument and the Jefferson Memorial. It is the same view every president has from the rear windows of the White House. Who, I wondered, would be the next occupant? A woman, perhaps?

ADAM VAN DOREN
130 WEST 57TH STREET · 13-B
NEW YORK, NEW YORK 10019

August 16, 2014

Dear David,

You will be pleased to know that I finally made it to the White House. Because of security restrictions I did not get a chance to get very close, however. I settled for a location near the Zero-milestone marker in Presidents Park. The rear of the house is surrounded by trees and they frame the view of the south elevation. . . . After working

on my painting for a few hours, I took time out for a tour. The last time I had seen the interior of the White House was over forty years ago, when I

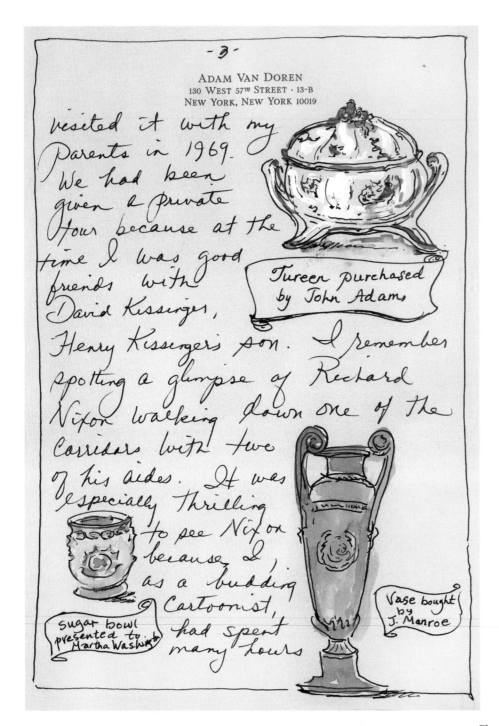

ADAM VAN DOREN
130 WEST 57TH STREET · 13-B
NEW YORK, NEW YORK 10019

visited it with my
Parents in 1969.
We had been
given a private
tour because at the
time I was good
friends with
David Kissinger,
Henry Kissinger's son. I remember
spotting a glimpse of Richard
Nixon walking down one of the
corridors with two
of his aides. It was
especially thrilling
to see Nixon
because I,
as a budding
Cartoonist,
had spent
many hours

Tureen purchased
by John Adams

Vase bought
by
J. Monroe

sugar bowl
presented to
Martha Washington

I Pray Heaven To Bestow
THE BEST OF BLESSINGS ON
This House

And ALL that shall hereafter inhabit it
May none but HONEST and Wise
Men ever rule under
This Roof
—John
Adams

making caricatures of him, with
his distinctive nose and high
forehead.
My most recent tour included
the Principal chambers, including
the Red Room, the State Dining Room,
The Green Room, The Queens Bedroom
and the Blue Room. This time
I did not see any president, but
I tried to imagine what it would

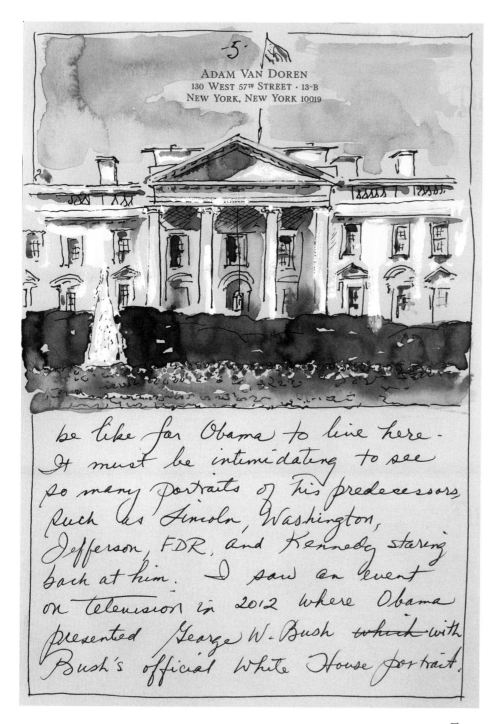

be like for Obama to live here.
It must be intimidating to see
so many portraits of his predecessors,
such as Lincoln, Washington,
Jefferson, FDR, and Kennedy staring
back at him. I saw an event
on television in 2012 where Obama
presented George W. Bush which with
Bush's official White House portrait.

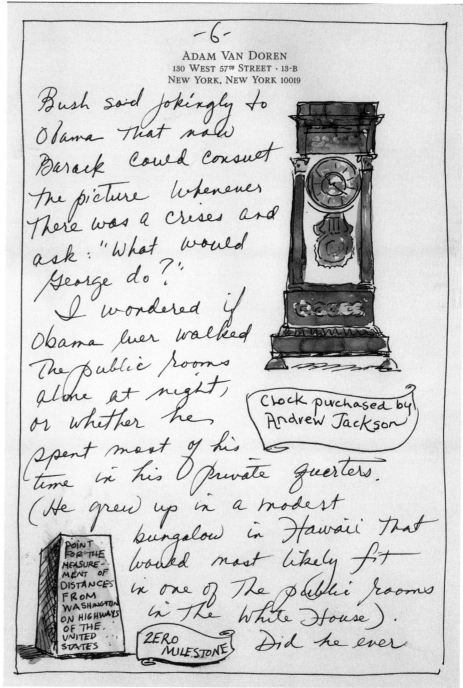

Bush said jokingly to
Obama that now
Barack could consult
the picture whenever
there was a crises and
ask: "What would
George do?"
I wondered if
Obama ever walked
the public rooms
alone at night,
or whether he
spent most of his
time in his private quarters.
(He grew up in a modest
bungalow in Hawaii that
would most likely fit
in one of the public rooms
in the White House).
Did he ever

Clock purchased by
Andrew Jackson

POINT
FOR THE
MEASURE-
MENT OF
DISTANCES
FROM
WASHINGTON
ON HIGHWAYS
OF THE
UNITED
STATES

ZERO
MILESTONE

ADAM VAN DOREN
130 WEST 57TH STREET · 13-B
NEW YORK, NEW YORK 10019

A. Lincoln

Four score and seven years ago our fathers brought forth, upon this continent, a new nation, conceived in Liberty, and dedicated to the proposition that all men are created equal.

Now we are engaged in a great civil war, testing whether that nation, or any nation, so conceived and so dedicated, can long endure. We are met on a great battlefield of that war. We have come to dedicate a portion of it as as a final resting place for those who here gave their lives that that nation might live. It is altogether fitting and proper that we should do this.

But in a larger sense we can not dedicate, we can not consecrate - we can not hallow this ground. The brave brave men, living and dead have consecrated at far above our poor power...

copy of Gettysburg address which hangs in Lincoln Bedroom

ADAM VAN DOREN
130 WEST 57TH STREET · 13-B
NEW YORK, NEW YORK 10019

Portrait of Ben Franklin by D. Martin

have time to appreciate the landscapes on the wall or the historic furniture that adorn the rooms? Or was he instead constantly being shuffled from one meeting to another, too busy to spontaneously sit and relax in one of the Empire-Style cushioned chairs and enjoy a good book.

FDR apparently enjoyed many candled moments in the White House. One scene was Portrayed in the Ken Burns's new documentary on The Roosevelts. Winston Churchill was visiting Franklin in the winter of 1943, and Roosevelt, anxious to deliver some good news to Winston, barged into the bathroom where the Prime Minister was nude in the bathtub. FDR apologized

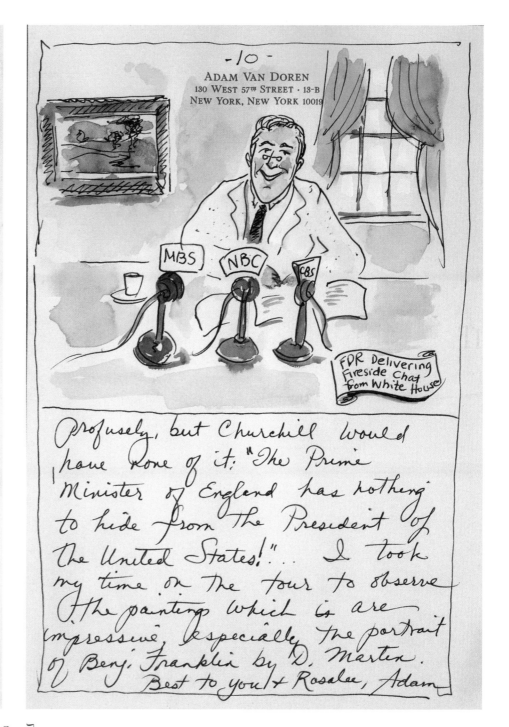

MBS NBC CBS

FDR Delivering
Fireside Chat
from White House

profusely, but Churchill would have none of it: "The Prime Minister of England has nothing to hide from the President of the United States!"... I took my time on the tour to observe the paintings which is are impressive, especially the portrait of Benj. Franklin by D. Martin.
Best to you & Rosalee, Adam

BRIEF BIOGRAPHIES OF THE PRESIDENTS

George Washington (1732-1799)
Mount Vernon, VA
(terms of office: 1789-1793; 1793-1797)

A veteran of the French and Indian War and the American Revolution, the father of our country was also president of the Constitutional Convention. On his substantial estate, which includes a twenty-one-room residence, he harvested wheat, corn, hemp, and flax. He and his wife Martha are buried on the property, which is owned and managed by the Mount Vernon Ladies Association. For more information, visit www.mountvernon.org.

John Adams (1735-1826)
Quincy, MA
(term of office: 1797-1801)

Trained as a lawyer, Adams defended British soldiers on trial for the Boston Massacre and later was instrumental in helping draft the Declaration of Independence. He served as vice president under Washington. His home at Peacefield, located only a mile from where he was born, contains many of his and his wife Abigail's original furnishings. A stone building on the property contains the library of his son John Quincy.

Thomas Jefferson (1743-1826)
Charlottesville, VA
(terms of office: 1801-1805; 1805-1809)

Thomas Jefferson, the principal author of the Declaration of Independence, was America's first Secretary of State. He was a proponent of religious freedom, founder of the University of Virginia, and the force behind the Louisiana Purchase and the Lewis and Clark expedition. His estate at Monticello is known for its Georgian brick architecture, its elaborate gardens, and its superior art collection. For more information, visit www.monticello.org.

James Madison (1751-1836)
Montpelier, VA
(terms of office:1809-1813; 1813-1817)

The father of the Constitution, Madison was Secretary of State under Jefferson and commander in chief during the War of 1812 when the White House burned. His ancestral home, with two chimneys and a low-hipped roof, was once the largest brick dwelling in Orange County and is now a historic site. For more information, visit www.montpelier.org.

James Monroe (1758-1831)
Charlottesville, VA

(terms of office: 1817-1821; 1821-1825)

A major in the Continental Army during the Revolutionary War, Monroe negotiated the Louisiana Purchase and was president during the Missouri Compromise. His 3,500-acre Ash Lawn-Highland estate, only a few miles from Jefferson's house, is now owned by The College of William and Mary and is open to the public. For more information, visit www.ashlawnhighland.org.

John Quincy Adams (1767-1848)
Quincy, MA

(term of office: 1825-1829)

The son of John Adams, John Quincy was an opponent of slavery and served in Congress following the presidency. As a young boy he studied in Paris and started a diary that he would continue for the next sixty years. He was born in the clapboard house where his father's first law office was located. His son Charles Francis Adams served in the House of Representatives, and his great grandson Henry Adams became a prominent historian. For more information, visit www.nps.gov/adam.

Andrew Jackson (1767-1845)
Nashville, TN

(terms of office: 1829-1833; 1833-1837)

Known as Old Hickory, Jackson was a populist president and the hero of the Battle of New Orleans. The Greek Revival Hermitage is a grand mansion with ten Doric columns, a rear portico and flanking wings. Much of the furniture and artifacts are original, and the site is one of the most visited presidential homes. For more information, visit www.thehermitage.com.

Martin Van Buren (1782-1862)
Kinderhook, NY

(term of office: 1837-1841)

Van Buren served as a senator and attorney general of New York before being appointed vice president during Andrew Jackson's administration. His estate in Kinderhook, New York, is a National Park site and is notable for its high Italianate architecture. Van Buren enjoyed entertaining large gatherings and completed several renovations of his homestead. For more information, visit www.nps.gov/mava.

William Henry Harrison (1773-1841)
Vincennes, IN

(term of office: March-April 1841, died in office)

Harrison was a major general during the War of 1812 and served in the House and the Senate. Harrison arranged several treaties with the Indians to open lands for white settlement. His mansion Grouseland, a National Historic Landmark, consists of a two-story red brick home where Harrison lived as governor of the Indiana Territory. The house was named for the plentiful grouse that inhabited the area. For more information, visit www.nps.gov/nr/travel/presidents/harrison_grouseland.html.

John Tyler (1790-1862)
Charles City, VA

(term of office: 1841-1845)

After serving in the House and Senate, Tyler was vice president under William Henry Harrison. A socially prominent Virginian, he called slavery a "dark cloud," but still managed to own seventy slaves. His Greek Revival Sherwood Forest Plantation was thought to be the longest frame house in America, at over three hundred feet long, and includes a seventy-foot ballroom for dancing the Virginia Reel. The house is open to the public. For more information, visit www. sherwoodforest.org.

James K. Polk (1795–1849)
Pineville, NC
(term of office: 1845–1849)

A former Speaker of the House and governor of Tennessee, Polk was commander in chief during the Mexican-American War. He created a separate treasury, annexed Texas, and acquired the California Territory. His log cabin birthplace is a replica and sits on twenty-one of its original 150 acres. "It was here," he wrote, "that I received lessons . . . which I attribute to whatever success has attended me." For more information, visit www.nchistoricsites.org/polk.

Zachary Taylor (1784–1850)
Louisville, KY
(term of office: 1849–1850, died in office)

A career officer, Taylor served in the War of 1812, the Black Hawk War, and the Mexican-American War. He hailed from a prominent family from the South and was a great advocate for the preservation of the Union. He spent most of his formative years at his four-hundred-acre family farm Springfield, where he is buried. The house, privately owned, contains a large dining room and a kitchen dating from 1790. For more information, visit www.nps.gov/nr/travel/presidents/zachary_taylor_springfield.html.

Millard Fillmore (1800–1874)
Moravia, NY
(term of office: 1850–1853)

A former schoolteacher and lawyer, Fillmore served in Congress before becoming vice president under Zachary Taylor. Fillmore was a moderate on slavery and signed the Compromise of 1850. He was born in a log cabin, which he described as "completely shut out from the enterprises of civilization and advancement." The house is owned by the Millard Fillmore Memorial Association. For more information, visit www.nps.gov/nr/travel/presidents/millard_fillmore_house.html.

Franklin Pierce (1804–1869)
Concord, NH
(term of office: 1853–1857)

A former lawyer and senator, Pierce was a lifelong friend of Nathaniel Hawthorne. As president, he sought to preserve the Union and helped engineer the purchase of a large portion of Mexico. "Elections are won by men and women," he wrote, "chiefly because most people vote against somebody rather than for somebody." His home is a distinguished clapboard house, open to the public and operated by the Pierce Brigade, a volunteer group. For more information, visit www.piercemanse.org.

James Buchanan (1791–1868)
Lancaster, PA
(term of office: 1857–1861)

A former minister to Russia and Britain, Buchanan was president during the Dred Scott case, in which the Supreme Court ruled that no person of African ancestry, enslaved or not, could be an American citizen, and therefore had no constitutional rights. "What is right and what is practicable," wrote Buchanan, "are two different things." His house Wheatfield is a substantial red brick structure with white trim. For more information, visit www.lancasterhistory.org.

Abraham Lincoln (1809-1865)
Springfield, IL
(term of office: 1861-1865, assassinated in office)

Born in a log cabin in Kentucky, Honest Abe rose from meager means to practice law, fight in the Black Hawk War, and serve in the House of Representatives. His presidency was marked by the Civil War and the signing of the Emancipation Proclamation. His Italianate house in Springfield has high ceilings and twelve rooms, and is open to the public. For more information, visit www.nps.gov/liho.

Andrew Johnson (1808-1875)
Greenville, TN
(term of office: 1865-1869)

After serving in the House, and then as governor of Tennessee, Johnson was one of the intended targets of the assassination plot that killed Lincoln. His administration focused on the reconstruction of the South but was derailed by his impeachment. His historic site includes two Johnson homes, his tailor shop, and his grave. The sixteen-acre property also includes a statue of the seventeenth president. For more information, visit www.nps.gov/anjo.

Ulysses S. Grant (1822-1885)
Galena, IL
(terms of office: 1869-1873; 1873-1877)

A hero of the Civil War (despite having been a poor student at West Point), Grant was a favorite of Lincoln's. As president, he fought to suppress the Ku Klux Klan and used federal troops to protect the freed former slaves. His Italianate house has projecting eaves supported by brackets and a low pitched roof. "I hope to retain my residence here," he wrote, "and I expect to cast my vote here always." For more information, visit www.granthome.com.

Rutherford B. Hayes (1822-1893)
Fremont, OH
(term of office: 1877-1881)

A general during the Civil War, Hayes served in the House and was governor of Ohio. His administration was hampered by an economic depression and several national labor strikes. His thirty-one-room mansion Spiegel Grove includes a notable staircase and a cupola with a greenhouse. Many artifacts have remained in the house including framed photographs of Lincoln. For more information, visit www.rbhayes.org/hayes/hayeshouse.

James Garfield (1831-1881)
Mentor, OH
(term of office: 1881, assassinated in office)

Raised by his widowed mother from the age of two, Garfield studied classics at Williams College and fought in the Civil War as a brigadier general. He served nine terms in the House, and worked toward civil service reform but was fatally shot 200 days into his first term. Garfield's home Lawnfield, from which the president ran a successful front porch campaign in 1880, is a National Historic Site. The home is a great example of Stick Style architecture. His wife Lucretia continued to live at the residence until her death in 1918. For more information, visit www.nps.gov/jaga.

Chester A. Arthur (1829-1886)

Fairfield, VT

(term of office: 1881-1885)

The son of a Baptist minister, Arthur studied law in New York. His administration was noted for strengthening the U.S. Navy, suspending Chinese immigration, and establishing the Civil Service Commission. A man of the Gilded Age, Arthur hired Louis C. Tiffany to help decorate the White House. His boyhood home was a modest cottage of which only a replica, open to the public, remains. For more information, visit historicsites.vermont.gov/directory/arthur.

Grover Cleveland (1837-1908)

(terms of office: 1885-1889; 1893-1897)

The only president to serve two non-consecutive terms, Cleveland was the governor of New York and the only chief executive to be married in the White House. He was a fiscal conservative who intervened in the Pullman strike. "Honor lies in honest toil," he once said. Westland, his former stone mansion in New Jersey, is not open to the public.

Benjamin Harrison (1833-1901)

Indianapolis, IN

(term of office: 1889-1893)

A former general in the Civil War, Harrison ran a famous "front porch" campaign from his residence, often drawing large crowds on the street. During his presidency, he signed the Sherman Antitrust Act to curb monopolies. His Victorian home has an ornate cornice, large bays, and an impressive staircase. For more information, visit www.presidentbenjaminharrison.org.

William McKinley (1843-1901)

Canton, OH

(terms of office: 1897-1901; 1901-1901; assassinated in office)

A major in the Civil War and a two-term governor of Ohio, McKinley was president during the Spanish-American War and was assassinated by an anarchist in 1901 while at the Buffalo Pan-American Exposition. His campaign slogan for his second term was "A full dinner pail." His original two-story home is gone, but a replica was built on the same site and is open to the public on the first weekend of each month from September to May. For more information, visit mckinleymuseum.org.

Theodore Roosevelt (1858-1919)

Oyster Bay, NY and New York, NY

(terms of office: 1901-1905; 1905-1909)

A sickly child, Roosevelt overcame frailty to fight in the Spanish-American War. He served in the Navy and became president following McKinley's assassination. TR expanded the powers of the executive branch and spearheaded the effort to build the Panama Canal. "Seize the moment—" he once said, "man was never intended to become an oyster." His boyhood townhouse in New York is a replica, but Sagamore Hill, his house in Oyster Bay, is original and full of personal effects. For more information, visit www.nps.gov/sahi.

William Howard Taft (1857-1930)

Cincinnati, OH

(term of office: 1909-1913)

A man with a varied political career, Taft was U.S. solicitor general, Chief Justice of the Supreme Court, dean of the University of Cincinnati

Law School, commissioner of the Philippines, and secretary of war under Roosevelt. As president he supported conservation of natural resources. His Greek Revival house, where he lived until he was appointed a professor of law at Yale Law School in 1913, is located in the suburbs of Cincinnati. For more information, visit www.nps.gov/wiho.

Woodrow Wilson (1856-1924)

Washington, DC

(terms of office: 1913-1917; 1917-1921)

A former college professor of history and political science, Wilson was the governor of New Jersey from 1911 to 1913. He was president during Prohibition and World War I and signed the first federal income tax bill. After he left office, he spent his last few years in a house in Washington, DC, which is open to the public. For more information, visit www.woodrowwilsonhouse.org.

Warren G. Harding (1865-1923)

Marion, OH

(term of office: 1921-1923; died in office)

A former newspaper publisher and U.S. senator, Harding's campaign enlisted 1920s celebrities including Al Jolson and Henry Ford. His presidency was embroiled in the Teapot Dome Scandal in which a cabinet member was sent to prison. Harding, a noted ladies man, lived with his wife Florence in a Queen Anne house that features original furniture and an expansive porch. The house is open to the public. For more information, visit www.hardinghome.org.

Calvin Coolidge (1872-1933)

Plymouth, VT

(terms of office: 1923-1925; 1925-1929)

Coolidge was governor of Massachusetts and vice president under Harding before entering the White House. He signed a bill restricting immigration, and his administration was known for reducing taxes. Coolidge was born in the small town of Plymouth, where his family owned a cheese shop. The two homes where Coolidge was raised and the shop are part of the historic properties that are open to the public. For more information, visit www.nps.gov/nr/travel/presidents/calvin_coolidge_homestead.html.

Herbert Hoover (1874-1964)

West Branch, IA

(term of office: 1929-1933)

A former mining engineer and entrepreneur, Hoover became a millionaire by 1914. He had been president for only seven months when the stock market crash of 1929 occurred, and during the Depression he opposed direct federal aid to the poor. He was raised in a tiny house measuring fourteen by twenty feet; the house is open to the public. "This cottage where I was born," Hoover wrote, "is physical proof of the unbounded opportunity of American life." For more information, visit www.nps.gov/heho.

Franklin Delano Roosevelt (1882-1945)

Hyde Park, NY

(terms of office: 1933-1937; 1937-1941; 1941-1945)

A former governor of New York and assistant secretary of the Navy, FDR served longer than any other president. Despite being stricken with polio, he was a steadfast leader throughout the Depression and World War II. His home at Springwood, which now includes the FDR library, was a happy constant in his life. It is now a National Park site and open year round. For more information, visit www.nps.gov/hofr.

Harry S. Truman (1884-1972)

Independence, MO

(terms of office: 1945-1949; 1949-1953)

Truman served in the army during World War I before becoming a judge and later, senator. His presidency was marked by World War II and the atomic bomb. Noted initiatives include his support for the Marshall Plan, the founding of the United Nations, and the recognition of Israel. His home, now owned by the National Parks, is a tall Victorian structure with two columnar porches, prominent gables, and high windows. The majority of furnishings and decorative details are original. For more information, visit www.nps.gov/hstr/index.htm.

Dwight D. Eisenhower (1890-1969)

Abilene, KS

(terms of office: 1953-1957; 1957-1961)

Following service in World War I, "Ike" led the D-Day invasion and was appointed the supreme commander of NATO by Truman. His presidential administration was marked by the end of the Korean War, the McCarthy hearings, the use of troops to enforce desegregation, and the execution of the Rosenbergs as alleged spies for the Soviets. His boyhood homestead, where he lived until he enrolled at West Point, is now a museum and library, both open to the public. For more information, visit www.eisenhower.archives.gov.

John F. Kennedy (1917-1963)

Hyannis Port, MA and Brookline, MA

(term in office: 1961-1963, assassinated in office)

After serving in World War II, for which he was awarded a Purple Heart, JFK served in the House and Senate. His presidency was noteworthy for the creation of the Peace Corps and the support for NASA funding to reach the moon. Born into a prominent family on both sides, Kennedy was raised in two handsome homes in Brookline, MA, while summering at his parents' home in Hyannis Port. The house on Beals Street in Brookline is open to the public; the other is not. For more information, visit www.nps.gov/jofi.

Lyndon B. Johnson (1908-1973)

Stonewall, TX

(terms of office: 1963-1965; 1965-1969)

After serving in the Navy in World War II, LBJ served in the House and Senate. Assuming the presidency after JFK's assassination, he signed a sweeping civil rights bill and declared a war on poverty. The LBJ Ranch, known as the Texas White House, was where he was born and died. His wife "Lady Bird" continued to live there until 2007. The site is open to the public. For more information, visit www.nps.gov/lyjo.

Richard M. Nixon (1913-1994)

Yorba Linda, CA

(terms in office: 1969-1973; 1973-1974)

After serving in the Navy and later the House and Senate, Nixon as president forged new relations with China, but his administration was marred by the Watergate scandal, which caused him to resign. His boyhood home was made from a kit by his father, a member of the Quaker community, and features clapboard siding and a low pitched gable roof. For more information, visit www.nps.gov/nr/travel/presidents/nixon_birthplace.html.

Gerald R. Ford (1913-2006)
East Grand Rapids, MI
(term of office: 1974-1977)

A representative of his Michigan district in Congress for twenty-five years, Ford is most remembered for his controversial decision to pardon Nixon, which cost him the election in 1976. His historic site is open to the public and includes a garage where he used to play penny ante poker with his friends. "It was a great hideaway," Ford wrote, "because my parents wouldn't climb the ladder to the second floor—or so I thought." For more information, visit www.fordlibrarymuseum.gov.

James Carter (1924-)
Plains, GA
(term of office: 1977-1981)

Born to a religious family in rural Georgia, Carter served in the Navy before becoming governor of his home state. His presidency was noted for a Middle East peace plan and for recognizing the People's Republic of China, but also for the Iran hostage crisis. Carter's boyhood home, a National Parks site, is a modest house located only a mile from his current residence. Carter has authored many books since the White House and frequently teaches Sunday school at his local church.

Ronald Reagan (1911-2004)
Tampico, IL and Dixon, IL
(terms of office: 1981-1985; 1985-1989)

A former Hollywood actor and governor of California, Reagan, "the Great Communicator," was known for tax cuts, increased defense spending, and limited government. "Government's first duty is to protect the people," he wrote, "not run their lives." He was born in a small apartment over a general store and later moved to a comfortable house in Dixon, one of the oldest river towns in Illinois. For more information, visit www.reaganhome.org.

George H. W. Bush (1924-)
(term of office: 1989-1993)

A former director of the CIA and a member of the House, Bush was also a World War II fighter pilot. He first settled in Midland, Texas, in a simple wood frame house, to begin work in the oil business. Bush was president during the Gulf War and the U.S. invasion of Panama. During his tenure, the Berlin Wall fell. "The totalitarian era is passing," Bush once said, "its old ideas blown away like leaves from an ancient, lifeless tree." His family home in Maine is not open to the public.

William J. Clinton (1946-)
Hope, AR
(terms of office: 1993-1997; 1997-2001)

After serving as attorney general of Arkansas, Clinton became governor of the state. As president during strong economic times, he reformed welfare and initiated a "Don't ask, don't tell" policy for the military. In the early 1950s, he lived at his boyhood home with his mother and stepfather and recalled later, "I still believe in a town called Hope." For more information, visit www.nps.gov/wicl.

George W. Bush (1946-)

(terms of office: 2001-2005; 2005-2009)

The son of a president, Bush was the owner of a major league baseball team and governor of Texas before being elected president in 2000. He presided over the wars in Afghanistan and Iraq, and said of 9/11: "This was not an act of terrorism, but an act of war." His support for AIDS relief was instrumental in halting its spread. Bush maintains two homes in Texas, neither of which is open to the public.

Barack H. Obama (1961-)

(terms of office: 2009-2013; 2013-present)

Born in Hawaii, Obama was a popular law professor and senator of Illinois before defeating John McCain for the presidency. His administration is noteworthy for the Affordable Care Act, the Economic Stimulus Act of 2008 that halted the Great Recession, and his efforts to end the Iraq War. His former homes in Hawaii and Chicago are not open to the public.

A GALLERY OF PRESIDENTS' HOMES

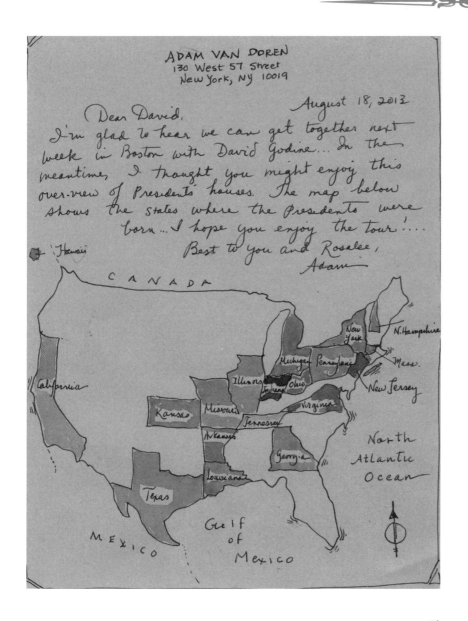

ADAM VAN DOREN
130 West 57 Street
New York, NY 10019

August 18, 2013

Dear David,
I'm glad to hear we can get together next week in Boston with David Godine... In the meantime, I thought you might enjoy this over-view of Presidents' houses. The map below shows the states where the Presidents were born... I hope you enjoy the tour'....
Best to you and Rosalee,
Adam

George Washington
Mount Vernon, VA

"..Washington was second to none in the humble and endearing scenes of private life..."
-"Lighthorse" Lee

John Adams
Quincy, Mass.

".. the beauties which my garden unfolds to my view from the window at which I now write... all unite to awaken the most pleasing sensation."
- Abigail Adams

John Quincy Adams

Madison settled on his 5,000 acre family farm in 1797 and was aknowlegd by Jefferson to be "America's best farmer..."

James Madison
Montpelier, VA

Monroe's farm encompassed 3,500 acres and included a saw mill, slave quarters, smoke house orchards, and vineyards

James Monroe
Ash-Lawn, Virginia

"Within a few days I retire to my family, my books, my farms... Never did a prisoner released from his chains feel such relief as I shall."
— T. Jefferson

Thomas Jefferson
Charlottesville, VA

John Quincy Adams called Martin Van Buren "l'ami de tout le monde," "the friend of all the world..."

Martin Van Buren
Kinderhook, N.Y.

John Tyler
Sherwood Forest

"I desire you to bear in mind three things: show no favoritism, accept no gifts, receive no seekers after office.
— J. Tyler

"With the union my best and dearest earthly hopes are entwined"
— F. Pierce

Franklin Pierce
Concord, N. Hampshire

"I believe that all the measures of the Government are directed to the purpose of making the rich richer and the poor poorer."
~ W. H. Harrison

William H. Harrison
Vicennes, Indiana

"I am heartily rejoiced that my term is so near its close. I will soon cease to be a servant and will become a sovereign."
J. Polk

James K. Polk
Pineville, N. Carolina

"One man with courage makes a majority."
~ A. Jackson

Andrew Jackson
The Hermitage

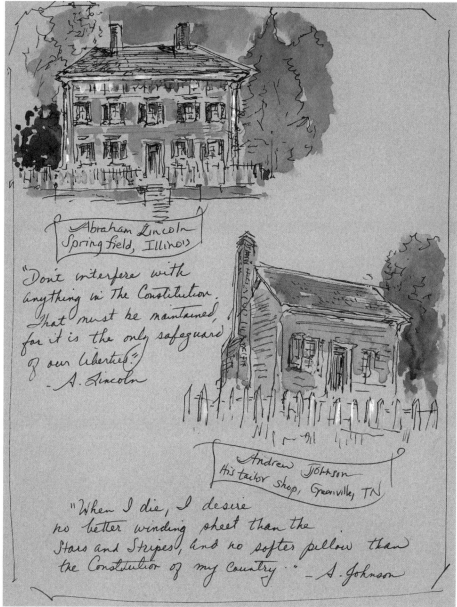

Abraham Lincoln
Springfield, Illinois

"Don't interfere with anything in the Constitution. That must be maintained, for it is the only safeguard of our liberties."
~ A. Lincoln

Andrew Johnson
His tailor shop, Greenville, TN

"When I die, I desire no better winding sheet than the Stars and Stripes, and no softer pillow than the Constitution of my country." ~ A. Johnson

When Ulysses S. Grant returned to Galena after the war in 1865, the citizens presented him and his wife with a new house as a symbol of their appreciation.

Ulysses S. Grant
Galena, IL

"If you are as happy entering the White House as I shall feel on returning to Wheatland, you are a happy man indeed."
— J. Buchanan

James Buchanan
Lancaster, Pennsylvania

"It is not strange to mistake change for progress." — M. Fillmore

Millard Fillmore
Moravia, New York

"I've always done my duty." — Z. Taylor

Zachary Taylor
Louisville, KY

"The filth and noise of crowded streets soon destroy the elasticity of health which belongs to the country boy." — R. B. Hayes

Rutherford Hayes
Fremont, Ohio

"If you are not too large for the place you occupy, you are too small for it."
— J. Garfield

James Garfield
Mentor, Ohio

"A truly American sentiment recognizes the dignity of labor and the fact that honor lies in honest toil." ~G. Cleveland

Grover Cleveland
Princeton, N. Jersey

"When a man receives the approbation of his neighbors, he is indeed blessed."
~ B. Harrison

Benjamin Harrison
Indianapolis, Indiana

"In the time of darkest defeat, victory may be the nearest..."
~ W. McKinley

William McKinley

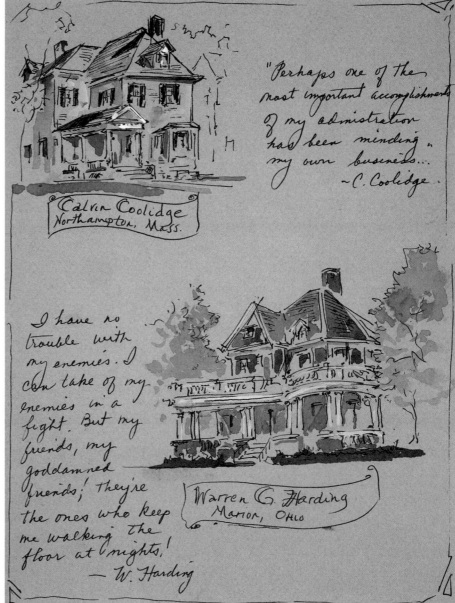

"Perhaps one of the most important accomplishments of my administration has been minding my own business..."
~ C. Coolidge

Calvin Coolidge
Northampton, Mass.

I have no trouble with my enemies. I can take care of my enemies in a fight. But my friends, my goddamned friends; they're the ones who keep me walking the floor at nights!
~ W. Harding

Warren G. Harding
Marion, Ohio

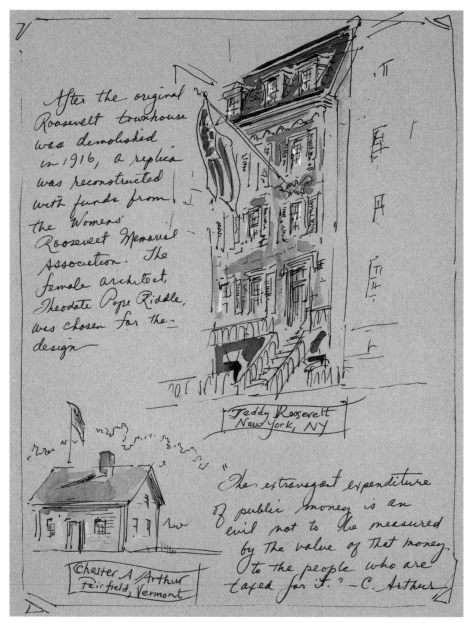

After the original Roosevelt townhouse was demolished in 1916, a replica was reconstructed with funds from the Womens' Roosevelt Memorial Association. The female architect, Theodate Pope Riddle, was chosen for the design

Teddy Roosevelt
New York, NY

Chester A Arthur
Fairfield, Vermont

"The extravagant expenditure of public money is an evil not to be measured by the value of that money to the people who are taxed for it." — C. Arthur

"I have long enjoyed the friendship and companionship of Republicans because I am by instinct a teacher, and I would like to teach them something..." — W. Wilson

Woodrow Wilson
Birthplace, Staunton Virginia

William H. Taft
Mount Auburn, Ohio

"We live in a stage of politics, where legislators seem to regard the passage of laws as much more important than the results of their enforcement."
— W. H. Taft.

"There are only two occasions when Americans respect privacy, especially in Presidents. Those are prayer and fishing."
— H. Hoover

Herbert Hoover
Birthplace, W. Branch, Iowa

"This is the house in which my husband was born... he always felt that this was his home." — Eleanor Roosevelt

Franklin D. Roosevelt
Hyde Park, New York

"It's a recession when your neighbor loses his job; it's a depression when you lose yours." — H. S. Truman

Harry S. Truman
Independence, Missouri

"I am the most religious man I know. Nobody goes through six years of war without faith."
— D. Eisenhower

Dwight D. Eisenhower
Abilene, Kansas

"...The righteousness of our cause must always underlie our strength..." — J. F. K.

J. Kennedy Compound
Hyannis Port, MA

Lyndon B. Johnson
Texas Hill Country

"Every man has a right to a Satnight Saturday night bath..."
— L. B. Johnson

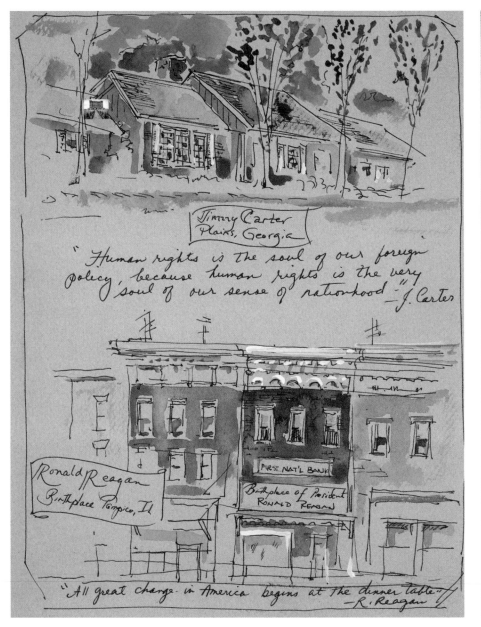

Jimmy Carter
Plains, Georgia

"Human rights is the soul of our foreign policy, because human rights is the very soul of our sense of nationhood." —J. Carter

Ronald Reagan
Birthplace Tampico, IL

FIRST NAT'L BANK

Birthplace of President RONALD REAGAN

"All great change in America begins at the dinner table." —R. Reagan

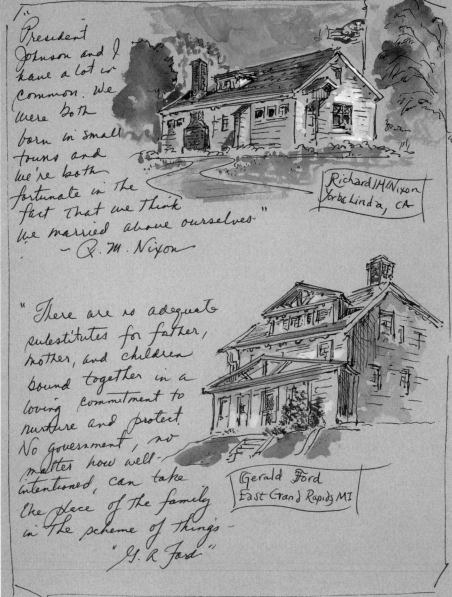

"President Johnson and I have a lot in common. We were both born in small towns and we're both fortunate in the fact that we think we married above ourselves." —R. M. Nixon

Richard M. Nixon
Yorba Linda, CA

"There are no adequate substitutes for father, mother, and children bound together in a loving commitment to nurture and protect. No government, no matter how well-intentioned, can take the place of the family in the scheme of things." "G. R. Ford"

Gerald Ford
East Grand Rapids MI

"Politics is just like show business. You have a hell of an opening, coast for a while, and then have a hell of a close."
— R. Reagan

Ronald Reagan
Dixon, Illinois

George W. Bush
Childhood Home
Midland, TX

"I have opinions of my own, strong opinions, but I don't always agree with them."
— G. H. W. Bush

"I came of age believing that, no matter what happened, I would always be able to support myself."
— B. H. Clinton

Bill Clinton
Hope, Arkansas

"There's not a liberal America and a conservative America — there's the United States of America."
— B. Obama

Barack Obama
Chicago, IL

"Americans are rising to the tasks of history, and they expect the same of us."
— G. W. Bush

George Bush
Walker Point, Maine

ACKNOWLEDGMENTS

THIS BOOK would not have been completed without the help of certain individuals who were more than generous with their time and insights. Special recognition goes to those who offered to read and edit the manuscript, including Alex Griffith, Byron Dobell, Sidney Offit, Paula Cooper, John Van Doren, and Susan Barba. I am grateful to those who assisted in gaining permissions to these houses and who provided valuable information and instructive tours, including James Shea of the Edward M. Kennedy Institute for the United States Senate, former Governor Bob Graham, Leslie Greene Bowman and Ann Lucas of the Thomas Jefferson Foundation, and biographer David Michaelis. Curators and National Parks rangers who gave generously of their expertise and time include Patrick Clarke, John Stanwich, Kelly Cobble, Kevin Thomas, Jim Roberts, Dawn Olson, Sarah Andrews, John Dumville, Robert Enholm, and Jeffrey Wade. I am extremely appreciative of the assistance provided by the United States Secret Service and the personal assistants of the living presidents, whose homes I visited, especially Audrey Akers, Logan Dryden, Hutton Hinson, Beth Davis; and of course, the presidents and first ladies themselves: Jimmy Carter, George W. and Laura Bush, and George H. W. and Barbara Bush, who welcomed me into their homes and allowed me the honor of becoming acquainted with them. Barnard College Professor James Basker and Lesley Herrmann of The Gilder Lehrman Institute of American History were generous with their support and interest, as was Vassar College Professor Richard Wilson, who loaned me a valuable audio recording of Eleanor Roosevelt. I am grateful to my son Henry who joined me on several of the visits, to Mira Van Doren for offering thoughtful ideas, and to my wife Charlotte and daughter Abbott who remained enthusiastic about the project throughout. I am indebted to Susan Ramin who encouraged me to submit the proposal for this book, and to David Godine and the book designer Jerry Kelly, whose extraordinary knowledge, taste, and vision were invaluable. I would also like to thank my students at Yale College who inspire me each year, Roger Angell of *The New Yorker* who had an engaging story for each president, Rosalee McCullough who was always full of helpful suggestions, and finally David McCullough for his valued friendship and thoughtful foreword to this book.

THE HOUSE TELLS THE STORY

has been typeset in Bell with Fry's Ornamented initials.
The Bell type was first cut by Richard Austin for the British publisher John Bell.
It fell into disuse before being re-discovered by D. B. Updike and Bruce Rogers,
both of whom used it at The Riverside Press in Cambridge, MA, and also in
their later work. An excellent adaptation was made under the supervsion
of Stanley Morison at the British Monotype Company.
The version you are now reading is a modification
of Monotype's digital rendering.
Book design & typography
by Jerry Kelly.